REBECCA THE LURCHER

Andrew Simpson

REBECCA THE LURCHER

Photographs by Fay Godwin

BARRIE & JENKINS
LONDON

Photographs printed by Chris Cox

First published by Barrie & Jenkins Ltd.
24 Highbury Crescent, London N5 1RX

Photoset in 12 on 15 point Photon Baskerville and Printed
by Redwood Press Limited
Trowbridge, Wiltshire

ISBN 0 214 66859 2

For me it all begins with Dinah, who is half Scottish deerhound and half greyhound. She is a long, strong dog, and big enough to nudge a tall man in the small of the back with her nose, without standing on tiptoes (she does it all the time). Her colour seems to me to be the same brindled grey-green of a tabby cat, and her coat, without being very long, is thick and wiry. At her neck, it fluffs out into a handsome ruff of a mane (now grey with age, as is her nose), and there are feathers above her hocks. (Do dogs have hocks? Do dogs have feathers? Anyway, the upper part of her hind legs is clothed in long hair.) Her head is deerhound, without being quite as broad as a pure deerhound, and she has fine brown eyes. All in all, she is most handsome. When she canters, she has an easy, rhythmic, flowing action: if you saw a two-year-old going down to the post moving like she does, you would not be wrong to back it.

Dinah was mated with a greyhound and had a family (consequently, the pups were three-quarters greyhound, one-quarter deerhound). They were in great demand, for Dinah's beauty was widely admired, and those that were disposed of went to the best of homes. One went to a veritable castle in Devon, with acres of lawn and a ha-ha running all the way round the house; another went to live with an illustrious racehorse-trainer in Kent—a man who 'snatched' many important prizes in his career, and nobody ever quite knew when or where he was going to pounce (long may he continue to flourish). A third went to a jockey in the New Forest, and in the course of time it hunted and killed several deer. The one that was kept was Spider (an odd name for a dog, but a name is no worse than the dog it belongs to). From her mother she inherited her height and her colour and her great depth through the heart, also her tail, which sloped down away from her body and then curved up in a loop behind her. She had her father's lean, flat head and wasp waist and racy hind legs, and his fine silky coat. When she met someone she liked she would wag her tail, and scrape her hind feet, and curl back her lips all the way round, revealing all of her teeth in the merriest grin I have ever seen. It had to be a grin because she only produced it when she was pleased. This she owed to neither of her parents, nor so far as I know to any of her ancestors; it was her own thing.

One afternoon—I know it was sunny, I think it was early autumn—Spider and Icy the whippet and I went walking on Kimpton Down gallops. As you start to walk along the main part of the gallops, you have a shoulder of a hill on your left hand, stretching as far as the eye can see till it loses itself in the hills above Salisbury Plain. Along the bottom—it is very steep—runs the gallop, like a river of bright green smooth turf, about three-quarters of a mile long and two hundred yards wide. Along the middle of it, at intervals of about a hundred yards, are big black bushes, planted many years ago. These have helped generations of work-riders to know which part of the gallop to use, how far to go, and where to change gear (or whatever the racing equivalent is). On the right, there is a wood, then plough, then a field of grass with trees growing in it (they look like apple-trees to me, but I'm sure they're not) then thick gorse and the beginnings of tank country. Perham Down Ranges are not far away in that direction.

We were walking along enjoying the weather on the right-hand side of the gallop. First we had woods on our right; then the woods were behind us and the plough began. We were almost at the end of it, when it happened: Spider's head went up, she took two strides and floated over four strands of wire and sped across the plough. I looked ahead of her, and saw a big hare "footing it nimbly". They went diagonally across the field, through an open gateway, and out of sight. Icy went in pursuit, and I began to clamber clumsily over the wire. Gumboots-across-plough is not a method of travel calculated to make one feel that one is flying and few things emphasise man's lack of pace so much as a hare and a fast dog. By the time I reached the gateway—and I thought I would never reach it—I was puffing and blowing and stumbling all over the place. I stopped and tried to get my breath back, but I never had a chance: the hare reappeared and hurtled towards me with Spider three yards behind, head down, covering the ground in great liquid strides. They passed ten yards from me; the hare dived through a wire fence. Spider half checked in her stride, lifted her head, measured the obstacle, soared into the air, and landed galloping. She had lost two yards, but she made it up by the time they had flashed through the trees and reached the far side. Another fence, and the hare was through, and once again Spider checked, looked and flew. They were on the gallops; the hare turned along them and went past one bush and then a second, but now Spider was at his tail; he squealed and turned back on his heels. The dog skidded round like a motor-cycle broadsiding, not losing her legs or her balance and very little of her momentum. Ten giant strides back towards me; then her lean head dipped, and her teeth shut on the back of his neck. I walked over and Icy was there helping. I killed the hare quickly because they hadn't, and I told Spider how clever she was, and Icy too. Then we walked home. It was a heavy hare, and I was full of exultation. I felt sure that the hillside and the woods, the plough and the gallops were all as happy and excited as I was, for it was a very thrilling experience. (In the cold light of reason I have to admit that the last few lines are so much nonsense, but that's how it seemed to me at the time.) The only sad thing was that the hare was never eaten. I gave it to my hostess (they were her dogs, and it was killed on her land), it was hung and then forgotten. I think that what one kills ought to be eaten (by the dog, if not by the master, and preferably by both). Otherwise the whole thing becomes pointless, at least it does for me. For me, it's no problem because I love jugged hare, and Rebecca is nuts about hare in any state, form or condition.

The jugging of a hare is a religious mystery that I prefer to leave to the experts. However, I have a tale to tell concerning the length of time it should be allowed to hang before being cooked. Some time ago, in a country restaurant of high repute, a friend and I went nap on the hare. It was very rich and very tasty and that night I had the most spine-chilling nightmares; next day my friend reported that he had had anything but a quiet night. A short time later Billy's owner (Billy will appear later on) asked me, quite out of the blue, if I had ever heard of hare causing nightmares. I told him what I knew and it transpired that the same thing had happened to him after eating a similarly well-hung, gamey hare. On the other hand, the best hare I ever had was caught on a Thursday (by Rebecca), cooked the following Tuesday, and eaten on the Wednesday. It was acclaimed as delicious by five people, and everyone slept well on it, including me and the friend who had shared my previous unpleasant experience. This leads me to suppose that hares haunt those that hang them too long. Who can blame them?

Spider died. She was two and a half years old. One day she was missing. A week later she was found dead in a field. It seemed likely that she had eaten something poisoned. Fate plays some particularly nasty tricks from time to time, and there is nothing one can do about it; this was one of them. Spider gave me my first glimpse of coursing, and I missed her; soon afterwards I got the idea that I would like a hare-catching dog of my own.

1

What is a lurcher? A question I am totally unqualified to answer, being, as I am, only a first-year student of this complex subject. (Beware of first-year students; they are full of woolly theories and wild imaginings. They do not yet know the value of hard facts and practical experience.) Still, I have posed the question, I must try to answer it. Once, in a glossy magazine, I saw the term 'dinner-snatcher' used to describe, or rather to define, a lurcher. It is not an expression I could imagine using myself. In fact, if I were to catch myself saying 'hello, my darling dinner-snatcher', I should feel very foolish, and I am sure Rebecca would be most embarrassed. However, it's not bad: a lurcher is a dog that is bred and trained to forage for his master and for himself. With the emphasis on the "snatching", for the lurcher is expected to do his job without begging a by-your-leave of anyone. He should be able to pounce on a pheasant, point at a partridge, pick up a rabbit, and outrun a hare. He should have the speed of a greyhound, the nose of a foxhound, and the eye of a hawk. Although built for speed, he should not flinch at thorns and thickets and barbed wire, nor at heavy plough underfoot, nor at the cold of long winter days and nights spent in the open. Although bred to hunt, he should be intelligent enough to learn not to worry sheep or chase cattle, and to be utterly still when

he is told to be utterly still. He may growl, but he should seldom bark. For him the eleventh commandment is 'Thou shalt not be caught.' In fact, a lurcher is a hungry poacher's dog, which is no easy role to play.

Lurchers come in all shapes and sizes; this is because they are always a mixture of at least two breeds, and often many more. No one breed has all the qualities required for the perfect lurcher, and so it is necessary to cross-breed, and cross-breed again and again in order to produce, ultimately, a dog with the many talents that are needed. For example, the greyhound has the speed, but seldom the nose or the intelligence. The deerhound has the constitution, but seldom the manoeuvrability. The whippet has the speed and the ability to turn quickly, but seldom the stamina. So lots of mixing goes on, and lurchers come in all the most extraordinary shapes and sizes. Some are very handsome, and some are positively grotesque. However, in order to qualify as lurchers, they have to pass a test; they have to be good at their job, which involves being strong and fast and athletic and cunning and loyal. A good lurcher is a dog which would keep his master alive, should all else fail. A bad lurcher just isn't a lurcher: he's simply a mistake. Nothing is further from my mind than to embroil myself in an argument between factions, but it does occur to me that the pure breeds of dogs, in contrast, are judged solely on their shape. Would the choice Chihuahua, one asks oneself, bring home the bacon for himself and his master, if ever the need arose? One simply does not know. However, that is another story, and *chacun à son gout,* and who am I to criticise other people because their idea of a dog is not the same as mine?

2

The Jockeys' Dance takes place at the beginning of the week before Christmas. There is seldom any racing that week: the jumping people enjoy a well-earned break, and the flat people are beginning to get pretty bored after two months of going round in circles; all departments are ready for their office party, which is roughly what the Jockeys' Dance is. Four or five hundred people congregate in the Stand at Newbury (the Stand is heavily disguised for the occasion). Racing is the one thing they all have in common. If a stranger, viewing the scene, were to point to a pretty girl and ask who she was, the answer would probably go something like 'That's Mildred Brown, Frank's daughter. Frank trained Bluebottle to win the Derby. That's Frank over there dancing with Daphne. Daphne is Sammy's wife. Sammy is one of Frank's lads. Sammy used to look after Bluebottle. That's Sammy in the corner knocking spots off the little man with the black eye. I think it's Snooks who used to ride Bluebottle. Sammy can never forgive him for getting beat in the St Leger. He thumps him every Christmas. That was a good one. Sent him right across the dance floor. He's landed on old Isaac's lap. Most appropriate. Why? Only because when Bluebottle lost the St Leger, Isaacs (he's a bookmaker) was said to have made a packet of money, and some of it (it is rumoured) rubbed off on little Snooks.' As with most office parties, it's business that brings the people together. Happily, the racing business has more than its fair share of attractive people. Even the baddies have a certain charm. When they congregate, a good time is had by all, including me, and this particular year I even won a prize at the Tombola, only I was too drunk to collect it. A few days later my friend Miss Brisket rang me up to tell me it had been lodged with a certain Mrs Burrows, and would I contact her and arrange to collect it.

I rang. 'Mrs Burrows?'
'Speaking.'
'Andrew Simpson. I hear you have a prize for me.'
'That's right. You must come and collect it.'
'What is it?'
'A carton of Goodboys.'
'Goodboys?'
'You must know . . .'
'I really don't . . .'
'They're chocolates.'
'Chocolates?'
'Chocolates for dogs.'
'For dogs?'
'Yes, you give them when they're good, and you say "Goodboy" (or "Goodboys" if there's more than one).'
'I see. What a coincidence.'
'Why?'
'Because I'm just looking for a dog. Perhaps this is an omen.'
'What sort of dog?'
'A hare-catcher.'
'What a coincidence.'
'Why?'

'We've just been offered one and we turned it down.'

'Tell me more.'

'It's a bitch puppy and both parents were good coursers.'

'Just what I want.'

'Are you serious?'

'Totally.'

'I'll ring the man, if you like.'

'Please do.'

'He's called James Mills. He lives near Faringdon. I'll ring him tonight. If you don't hear from me tomorrow, you'll know it's all right. Ring him and arrange to collect it. You'll find his number in the book. Winterton Farm.'

'Will it be expensive?'

'Free. He's got a litter, and he needs to find homes for them.'

'Cor, thank you very much.'

'Not at all. What about the Goodboys?'

'Why don't you keep them as a present? Call it commission on the deal.'

'Thank you very much.'

'Thank *you*.'

I think it was January 7th, in the afternoon, that I drove to Winterton Farm, near Faringdon, to collect Rebecca. My recollection is vague, but I seem to remember it was a dirty day. The road was wet and snow was on the ground, but not very deep, for the ridges of plough made black ragged lines across the fields. My recollection is vague, but I think I picked up a girl hitch-hiker outside Wantage, quite a pretty girl with fair hair and spots. She was a trainee nurse whose father had been the Vicar of Little Coxwell, or some such place. I can't remember what she was doing there that day, but we had a drink in a pub, and the landlord said 'Welcome back.' She knew the country and gave me directions to Winterton. My recollection is vague because at the time I wasn't concentrating on the journey, but on the hundred and one items of preparation that had intruded on my life since I spoke to James Mills and committed myself to dog-ownership. Mrs Gordon had given me the bed, so that was all right. I had the blanket, the feeding bowl, and the water bowl. I had the collar and the lead. The first-aid box was brimming with T.C.P., flea powder, bandages, and several types of worm-eliminator. Was it redworm, lugworm, or roundworm that I was most likely to run foul of? How did one tell one from the other? I had bought Saval I, Saval II, codliver oil, minced beef, and Farex. Breakfast consists of Farex and sugar in warm milk. Lunch is minced beef and Saval I in gravy. Have I got the Oxos? Tea is—what on earth is tea? Mrs Gordon certainly told me, but I can't remember. And it'll be tea-time when we get home. Oh tragedy! What a way to

start. I hope she's at home so I can phone her and find out. Mrs Gordon will save the day, I'm sure of it.

Mrs Gordon was, and is, a lovely lady whom I had had the good fortune to meet some months before. She is not very tall and on the broad side, and she is faultless apart from her laugh, which is loud and inclined to run away with her. She lives in a cottage with at least six whippets at any one time (and three children). She is an 'authority' on dogs, she knows everything and wins prizes. She had given me all my 'pre-natal' advice (I am sure that acquiring Rebecca was, for me, more of an ordeal than childbirth). She instructed me as to how I was to behave, and furnished me with lists of the essentials that would be needed. Wherever possible she gave me anything of hers that was surplus to her own requirements, like the bed. In the months to come she was to be a veritable angel; I used to ring her daily for advice, and when I began to bite my nails over something (which happened all the time) she would produce the answers and solve the problems. At least once a week I would take Rebecca round to see her, and she would scrutinise her and comment on her appearance and health and general progress, and do all the tricky things, like cutting her nails, worming and de-lousing her—all the things that I considered myself unqualified to do.

I felt such an impostor. Thirty-five and never owned a dog before, yet here I was. Had it been Battersea Dogs Home, and had I been about to save some wretched creature from being destroyed, it would have been all right. But I was driving into the palatial farmyard of a landed gent, and the dog I was about to appropriate was a high-bred lurcher, the sort of animal that landed gents distribute, carefully and after deliberation, among their land-owning peers. I suppose I was, after a fashion, the uncrowned lieutenant of several rolling acres (I worked in the office of a racing stable with its own gallops), but it wasn't enough, and I felt it.

'Nice cars, aren't they?' said Mr Mills. I looked at the Mini and despaired. If only I had a Landrover, full of mud and sacks and baler-twine. Or a shooting-brake with bits of saddlery in the back. Or a Rolls-Royce with a chauffeur. But no, I had an old mini with a twisted roof-rack. I began to hate myself.

'She's small, but she's the only one to get over that.' He was referring to 'my' dog and the bale of straw that barred the door of the loose-box in which she lived. 'We often find her in the yard in the morning.' He pushed the bale aside, and they came rolling and flopping out. I think there were five or six of them. All I can remember is that they were tiny and looked very helpless. I remember picking up 'my' one and feeling very awkward and talking earnestly about diet and suchlike and putting her down again as soon as I felt I decently could. She paddled back to the others. A bachelor uncle is always forgiven his clumsiness when first he handles his newborn nephew or niece, but I could not help feeling that in a would-be lurcher-owner such gaucheness was unpardonable.

'Half foxhound, half greyhound,' said Mr Mills. I had been looking with admiration at a very big, light chestnut dog. It was handsome, and didn't look like any dog I had ever seen before. 'Once killed six consecutive hares on his own.'

'Is that good?' I asked. I could have fractured my tongue the moment the words were uttered.

'It's not often done,' said he shortly.

Mother and father dog were there. They had a lot of the greyhound about their make and shape, but they were both a bit smaller than the average greyhound. Mother was very muscular and very attractive, her head and neck were white, her body brindle. Father was taller and leaner and dark brindle all over. Both had the same watchful expression in their eyes. They seemed to be continually looking at something, or for something, in the far distance. Maybe I imagined it. Maybe they were just looking straight through me because they disapproved of me as a prospective guardian for their smallest daughter. Who could blame them? However it was too late to turn back. I mentioned paying for her. 'Let me have a pup when you breed from her,' said Mr Mills. I found this rather heartening. He didn't think it was utterly impossible that she would survive long enough to become a mother. Full of new hope, I picked her up again and laid her tenderly on the newspaper on the front seat of the mini. (Mrs Gordon had said, 'Your puppy will probably be car-sick, especially on her first journey,' but Mrs Gordon was wrong for once; Rebecca has never been car-sick in her life.) Then I made my adieus and drove gingerly away.

She was seven weeks old, and tiny: one hand was all one needed to pick her up: one slipped the fingers under her bulbous little stomach and lifted; her head and front legs drooped down one side, her rear end hung down the other; she balanced very nicely. Her shape was, I imagine, the same as most seven week old puppies: her minute legs seemed quite incapable of supporting her weight: they splayed and collapsed if ever she tried to do more than a steady amble; her belly didn't often seem to clear the ground; her head was short, stubby, and puppylike. Her body was brindle: brown and black mottled together; three of her collapsible legs and all of her feet were white, as was the tip of her tail, and also her head, neck, and chest. Her left ear was brindle growing out of an isolated brindle splodge that covered that bit of her head: this gave her the look of a bit of a clown. Finally her eyes were pale blue. Rather weird they looked: washy pale blue exteriors, then a dark blue ring surrounding the black pupil. They gave her an almost menacing air when she stared at one: nobody I have yet met has ever seen a dog with eyes like hers.

3

I won't say much about Rebecca's character because I think it will speak for itself. I will simply write down some of the incidents in her life, which will gradually paint a far truer picture of her personality than any description of mine. Besides which, I am hopelessly biased. However, there is one thing about her that I must mention, because it deserves to be mentioned: her passionate love for her friends. She didn't make friends easily; her usual reaction was to back away from strangers, and to be most particular about who was allowed to touch, stroke, or pat her. Gradually, she built up a little group of people she admired: like Bernard and Anne (who owned Dinah), Stephen (who owned Maxwell), Paul and Mary (who owned Titus). When she met them, her joy knew no bounds. Her tail ran away with her body which flailed from side to side like a swinging gate in a high wind. She would go into acrobatic contortions to present them with their quota of licks and kisses and whispered sweet nothings. For her doggy friends she had two ways of saying 'Hello. How nice to see you.' Indoors, she would trot up for a quick wag, lick and sniff; then all concerned would take a lightning spin over every bit of furniture in sight. Outdoors, the moment she saw a friend she would drop on her belly and try to hide behind her forepaws; when 'friend' approached, she would

spring to her feet, side-step, and lead off for a grand
gallop round the countryside. With me, though I say it
myself, she was every bit as enthusiastic; this was most
gratifying, but at the same time rather embarrassing. For
example, we might spend the morning having row after
row, ending up with vicious blows on my part and angry
howls from Rebecca. Then perhaps I wouldn't see her for
an hour while I drove into town to do some chores. When

I got back, instead of the hostile reception I felt I deserved, I would invariably be engulfed in waves of amorous delight; she would throw herself at me, and knock my spectacles off, and moan passionately deep down in her throat. She made me feel a swine. However, the embarrassment didn't last long: her ability to infuriate me was far greater than her talent for making me feel guilty.

House-training was one of our first bones of contention. For a long time she remained world champion messer. In my diary I recorded twenty 'messes various' between May 6th and June 6th. These covered (I use the word advisedly) my home, my office, my car, my friends' homes, and in one case a bed in a friend's home.

The fault was entirely mine. It is true that she came from a long line of farmyard dwellers and had inherited no instinct for clean habits. It is true that she used 'messing' as a weapon of revenge when she felt she had been hard-done by. (I experienced this early on, the first time I walloped her for eating muck on the muckheap. She immediately galloped into the office and widdled on the mat in front of the electric fire.) It is true that in her extreme youth she suffered from some form of incontinence. How else does one explain the fact that she used to wet her own bed? Nevertheless I still think the fault was mine: some mornings I would get up early and 'walk' her for hours; other mornings I'd oversleep and she'd have two minutes if she was lucky. Some days we would walk on the downs at lunchtime; other days she would spend lunchtime in my car. In the evenings I was even worse: if she was lucky I would feed her, walk her, stay with her and walk her again extensively at bedtime. More often than not, however, I would come home in a terrible rush, feed her, lock her out while I bathed, and then shut her up while I went out, not to return till the early hours of the morning, when I would get into a frightful temper because she had messed. I was very ignorant and I confess it. The truth is, an impecunious bachelor, living alone, and inclined to forage abroad at night, should not be allowed to have a puppy; especially if he knows as little about dogs as I did. Now, I am proud to say, I am much wiser. I know, for example, that the early training of a young dog is facilitated, expedited, and enormously helped on its way if the puppy is surrounded by older dogs who can give a nod and a wink and a nudge in the right direction, not to mention a communal shiver of doggy distaste whenever junior makes a pig of himself. I couldn't be blamed for not having other dogs, but in every other way the *culpa* was exclusively *mea*. I should have fed her regularly and walked her, not only regularly, but for a long time and patiently, and I should have cunningly contrived it that she had no choice but to do the right thing at the right time at the right place. Then I should have shown my appreciation and rewarded her. Thus, in a matter of a few weeks, one would have created such a pattern of normal good behaviour that she simply would never have had the chance to learn how to conduct herself otherwise —that is to say, revoltingly. At the time I was too stupid to understand this; the revelation occurred later. When I moved from Darlingsford to Framfield, Rebecca and I found ourselves in the company of people who understood about dogs, and dogs who understood about people. Very soon both of us began to show marked improvement in our behaviour: the other dogs taught her that to scratch at the door and cough apologetically can be quite a smart thing to do, and the other people taught me how to interpret the signal. I'm sure she learned a lot quicker than I did. (Here endeth the washing of the dirty linen.)

I don't recall that anything particularly momentous occurred during January, February, March or April. We lived in a cottage at East Rediton (a thatched roof, three up and three down, a black Rayburn in the dining-room that never failed, and a garden that was never gardened. I can't speak too highly of the Rayburn: an empty warm cottage is so much nicer to come home to than an empty cold one.) We spent our days in the office and around the stable yard at Darlingsford. At weekends we would go over to Framfield, usually for Sunday lunch; I would have a mighty lunch, and Rebecca would exercise herself with the younger dogs under the watchful eye of Dinah, who was very quick to call them to order if ever their activities became too boisterous and disturbed her. At the cottage she had two friends. One was called Dusty; he was a Labrador-type puppy, about Rebecca's age, black with curiously grey feet. They spent a lot of time wrestling together in my garden and in the farmyard beyond. The other was called Midge—a little white terrier. To visit him (or her, I can't remember which) she had to go down the lane and cross the road. Whenever this happened I had heart-failure. In those early days I was always convinced that some terrible disaster was about to overtake her, and that I would be to blame. The first time that she got sick (vomited, that is), I rang the vet. He laughed, and later rang Mrs Gordon to tell her about it. She laughed, and later rang me, and explained that one of the nicest things about dogs is that, when they eat something that disagrees with them, they sick it up and that's the end of the matter. I was reluctant to believe that it could be so simple, but it was. About once a week we would make our little pilgrimage to Mrs Gordon's and ask her opinion about Rebecca's coat, her size, her weight, her diet, and every little incident that might have worried me during the previous seven days. She would laugh outrageously and work the oracle and set my mind at rest (and feed me), and Rebecca would spend an exhilarating hour being mercilessly bullied by all of her whippets. Rebecca, if the truth were known, never had a sick day in her life. She just ate and ate and ate, and grew and grew and grew.

In fact the only physical adventure that befell her during her childhood concerned her right ear. I noticed one day that when she pricked her ears the left one stood right up and looked very elegant; but the right one (the white one) only stood half up; the top half flopped down behind and made her look rather lopsided. I had not complained about the clownlike pigmentation of her head; but a lopsided ear was, I felt, going too far.

I consulted the experts and for once it wasn't Mrs Gordon who provided the answer. My friend Dr Hartington, a long-time breeder of some sort of tall fuzzy terrier, told me to paint the inside of the ear with colourless nail-varnish. I felt rather silly buying it in the chemists in Marlborough, but I was proud of the cunning I displayed in planning the actual operation. Instead of launching myself hot-foot at a reluctant and no doubt unco-operative Rebecca, I waited. I waited till she had had a particularly vigorous bout with Dusty and had stretched herself out in front of the fire to recover. As soon as she was snoring I moved into silent action. She never felt a thing. When she woke up, her ear had long since been painted. The varnish had set, the ear stood up very prettily, and has done so ever since.

I suppose this incident shows that I was beginning to learn a bit about dog-management. As the weeks went by, my knowledge increased. I could prepare her meals without constant reference to the inside cover of *Stable Management* (by Captain Horace Hayes), where it was all written out. I discovered that Farex and water and honey is better than Farex and milk and sugar; that minced beef can be served raw, while hearts and lights must be well cooked; that a raw egg added to anything turns a fastidious puppy into a ravening wolf; that when they start to 'crunch' their biscuit is the time to substitute Saval II for Saval I. Meanwhile Rebecca survived and flourished and waxed exceeding healthy.

4

Domestic life with Rebecca during those early months conformed, no doubt, to the immutable rules that govern the association of a dog like her with a man like me. It should have been simple enough; however, neither of us knew what these immutable rules were (she can hardly be blamed for this), and so there was always an awareness that the unexpected might happen, and that at any moment one might embroil oneself in labyrinthine difficulties, which one could have easily avoided if one had known better, but one didn't. The fault was mine, for I approached the dog-scene with a great deal too much intensity, and involvement. Intensity, involvement, and ignorance are not a very happy combination. My Mrs Chapel, who used to 'do' for me before I moved to the cottage (and who then did my laundry) said to Miss Battle (who inherited her valuable services when I moved), 'There won't be any courting for that Mr Simpson, not while he's got that dog.' A most damaging analysis, were it not completely justified. I admit that into the doggy-pitfall I fell as deep as it is possible for mortal man to fall. Naturally I regret and repent, and my resolutions for the future are of the best: to my next dog I will be friendly, attentive, and generous, but at the same time a trifle aloof. I shall be full of approbation when it is good, and a veritable hanging judge when it oversteps the mark, be it by however so little (I am not sure if that is English). Never again will a dog have me on the end of a string; and furthermore, if I ever again lose so much as a moment's sleep over a dog, I'll give it all up and confess that I'm hopelessly unsuited.

My memories from those early days are few but vivid. I remember attacking the overgrown, nettle-ridden, bramble-barricaded garden with a roto-mower. The first cut went fifteen or so yards into the jungle, past the yew tree, round the outside lavatory (now, thank God, purely ornamental), and fifteen yards back to the front door. I liked the look of what I had done, so I went over it again. Soon I had created a close-shaved track about two and a half feet wide, surrounded on all sides by jungle eighteen inches or more high. Rebecca loved it. She galloped round it. She skidded round it. She cartwheeled round it. She stole things from the house and made me chase her round it. I soon discovered that she had the edge as far as speed was concerned, so, once she was launched into orbit, I would throw myself down into the tall greenery, wait for her to complete a circuit, and ambush her. She adored it. She would wrestle and bite and kick with her legs in the air. Then she'd snatch up the shoe or the sock (or whatever it was we were fighting over) and gallop off with it back up the track. Usually I would retire to the house at about this stage, and she'd come after me, and taunt me till I roared at her and galloped in pursuit. Then she'd flee to the garden, disappear round the lavatory, and be ambushed as before.

I remember trying to create a kitchen garden. When I dug, she dug, which did no harm; in fact I suppose it helped a little. But when I sowed, she went on digging, which led to a certain amount of discord: I would hate to have to admit that she won the argument, but I must

admit that the kitchen garden was never a success.

I remember coming home to make breakfast after riding out first lot. Time was of the essence and I was well practised in the routine: kettle on, egg-pan on, grill on, toast inserted, tea-bags at the ready. Then table laid, toast buttered, tea made. Fill up egg-pan from electric kettle (electric kettle much faster than cooker, which, by this time, has rather brutally warmed up the bottom of the empty egg-pan). Let it boil: finally, in go the eggs. Only there weren't any eggs. Why weren't there any eggs? Because I had been giving Rebecca a raw egg in her dinner every night for God knows how long and the stock was exhausted. If there's one thing that depresses me—ruins the day even—it's breakfast with no egg. Still, whose fault was it? Why should the poor dog get sworn at?

I remember returning to my car after lunching in the pub to find Rebecca lying demurely on the back seat. She was behaving demurely because she had her mouth full; it was full of the corner of an envelope; the envelope should have been posted by me before lunch, rather than left with Rebecca during it; in the envelope were the relics of our monthly bill to our largest owner; it had been left till after the others were done because it was the biggest and most important and represented forty per cent of our monthly income, and took about three hours to calculate and prepare. Still, whose fault was it? Why should a puppy be chastised for chewing a delicious envelope that was left for three-quarters of an hour right under her moist and quivering nostrils?

I remember the afternoon that the grocer's man drove his van right into the stable-yard and parked just outside the office window. He then prepared to make his deliveries: first to the house, and then to the hostel (with a chat at each, and the possibility of a cup of tea if he was lucky). I went to the office door and remonstrated with him: Was it not the practice, hallowed by the continuity of countless years, that he should park outside the gates, and carry his parcels on foot to their various destinations? Was it not an offence against tradition (if nothing else) to open the gates through which he had just, so boldly, driven? What would happen if the horses decided to stream out of their locked boxes, into the locked passages, out into the yard, and thence onto the main road which he had so rashly made available to them? He made as if to move, demonstrated a palpable limp, explained that he was temporarily crippled, and undertook never to repeat the transgression. I returned to my desk, he returned to his business. He limped into the house with a parcel, whereupon, through my window, I saw Rebecca leap into the back of his van. I got up to call her off, but it was all right for she was out again before I had time to shout; only it wasn't all right, for in her mouth she had half a pound of Shaw's finest sliced ham. This she carried into the outer office and prepared to devour, obviously well pleased with herself. I suppose she reckoned I had been too soft with the man, and that she should take it upon herself to punish him properly. In a way I understood how she felt, but what on earth was I to do? Should I confess, and return the savaged ham to the very man to whom I had so recently been laying down the laws of good behaviour? Or should I lie low until he discovered the loss, raised the hue and cry, and eventually pinned the guilt on Rebecca? In which case I would be seen to be, not just an unlucky dog-owner, but a convicted accessory after the fact. In the event, I said nowt, and he noticed nowt, and Rebecca had the ham.

5

I first became aware of her hunting instincts one cloudy morning towards the end of March, or at the beginning of April. She came out with me onto the downs to watch the horses canter 'up the bank'. The bank is a three-furlong uphill stretch, which is divided into three strips. The first of these is hardly ever cut, and the grass grows thick and wild: sometimes in winter, when everywhere else is frozen hard, one can still canter horses there because there is so much grass that the ground remains soft and springy. The second strip is not quite so over-grown and is generally used in the early spring: it gets horribly churned up when the weather is wet, and is then given ten months off to recover. The third strip is particu-larly well looked after. It is here that the horses sprint the day before they run: a short sharp scamper to clear the cobwebs out of their lungs. I had Rebecca on a lead, and as the horses cantered up and passed in front of us, she began to pull against it, and leap in the air. She nearly strangled herself, she was so determined to go in pursuit. Only a tiny little thing, but when roused her strength was extraordinary. I gripped her by the collar, but that did very little good: eventually the only way I could control her was to squat down with her between my knees and both my hands round her neck. I was quite relieved to get her back into the van and return her to the safety of the office.

The next sign came a few days later. I was attempting to inspire one of the apprentices to work harder at his riding. (Far be it from me to pontificate on the subject of apprentices, but I must admit to nursing a suspicion that theirs is not a particularly happy lot. Luck plays a terrible large part in their lives, but even so the apprentice who sits on his backside and simply waits for success to tap him on the shoulder is in for a long wait indeed. They must work and work, and improve, and pester their masters for race-riding experience, and leave no stone unturned in their search for perfection.) That had been the burden of my song to this particular apprentice, whose name was Smith. So it came to pass that he and I rode out one fine afternoon, me on the old grey hack and him on the arthritic bay pony. We rode bareback, because that was what it was all about, and Rebecca came with us.

'We ride without saddles,' said I, 'because that helps to strengthen the grip of our legs. We ride with our legs hanging straight down, and we develop muscles, and then, when we start riding like jockeys with our knees right up by the horse's withers . . .' At this point I hoisted my knees up by the horse's withers; the horse resented the change and jumped sideways, and I landed in a heap on the ground. The conclusion of my lecture was, alas, lost in my confusion and Smith's unquenchable laughter.

Not the most propitious beginning, but we persevered, trotted all over the downs, did much good work, and sweated profusely. By the time we began to head for home I got him to agree that riding bareback was the key to success. (Such was the discomfort, I suspect he would have agreed to anything just to get it over and done with.) All this time Rebecca had been accompanying us,

and her behaviour had been faultless. We returned finally to the little paddock adjoining the stables. There was a
tree-trunk lying on the ground in one corner; the chance
of a final dramatic flourish was not to be missed. 'Follow
me,' said I, and I trotted round and popped over it.
Thereupon, the obstacle having been surmounted, I
found myself heading at an ever-increasing pace towards
the main road. The grey beast had gone berserk. At last I
managed to pull him round in ever-decreasing circles
(not so easy without a saddle), and he reluctantly slowed
down, but he would keep on snorting and prancing and
leaping. I then perceived the cause of the upheaval: the
vile blue-eyed one was hurling herself at his rear end as
though nothing else mattered. The air resounded with the
symphony of my rage (and fright) but it didn't do any
good. Finally, I baled out without much dignity, swung
the horse round so that I could get at the dog, and kicked
her as hard as I could. That stopped her for a while, and
I beat a hasty retreat to the yard. The boy was shouting
with mirth; when he recovered the faculty of speech he
told me that when I took off to jump the tree, Rebecca
took off and grabbed the hack's tail in her mouth, and
that she hung on all the time he was careering round the
paddock. It must have been a lovely sight, but the impli-
cations were fairly alarming: the beast seemed to have a
compulsion to pursue everything that moved, with no
regard for shape, size, species, race, colour, or creed. I
saw trouble ahead.

6

Slinford Down Farm is my favourite farm in all of England. To get to it, you take a narrow winding road out of the Yatesbury Vale, halfway up to the downs. Then you turn onto a 'No Through Road', go through the tiny village, and mount even higher. You reach the farm buildings, join the farm road, and climb steeply to the barn. If you stop and look back, you seem to be on top of the world: all the West of England lies at your feet. When you turn towards the East you realise you are only halfway there: rolling cornfields—bright green in April—stretch upwards to a wild gorsy ridge that is the summit of Slinford Down Farm. All around are broad shoulders of hillside, dropping precipitously into bottomless valleys that twist and spread in the strange pattern that the receding Ice Age left behind. (I'm guessing about the Ice Age; it's simply that the place looks as though it was carved by glaciers.) There are rivers of green corn along the bottoms, following the lines of the flat and arable land, surrounded by downland so precipitous that even the sheep need to watch where they walk. Up above, vast level cornfields, and at the top the ragged, savage, wind-swept ridge (the lair of pheasants, partridges, and hares) uncompromisingly defies the farmer. We went up there, Rebecca, Titus, Stephen, and I on the afternoon of April 25th, which was like the best sort of

June day. The sun shone down out of a clear sky, and whenever there was a lull in the proceedings we lay on the grass and smoked, without there ever being even the suggestion of a cold breeze; which is unusual, on high ground, in April, in England. Titus is a big, strong, fawn-coloured whippet. Very quiet and gentle, and mad about chasing hares; he always enjoyed coming out on expeditions with us. We thought we'd see if we couldn't find a hare for him to course, so that Rebecca could have a first look at the business of hunting. This was, I now realise, a diabolical liberty to take with a dog of her age, which was five and a half months; she shouldn't have been allowed to even think of hares till she was at least a year old, for fear of getting committed to an arduous hunt and straining her immature heart. All my friends had been unanimous that a dog should not be loosed off after a hare till it is a year or eighteen months old. I learned later that even track greyhounds are not permitted to gallop till they are a year old, when they go three hundred yards and no further. Besides all of this, it was April, when hares are hampered by the responsibilities of family life and sportsmen are expected to leave them alone. All in all, it was not a very good idea, but at the time it seemed irresistible.

We drove the Landrover as far as we could and then proceeded on foot. We were now on the 'middle ground', a very steep, wild hillside. It consisted of a series of deep little valleys ('re-entrants' is, I think, the proper term for them) cutting into the hillside, separated from each other by bulging shoulders of high ground (which, I think, are called 'spurs'). Above and below, miles and miles of the great wide arable. Our technique may well not be recognised by the more sophisticated coursers and poachers, but it was as follows: we decided to make our first effort on one of the fields on the high ground: so we made our way along the bottom of the rough, until we were directly below the chosen spot. Then we picked the nearest re-entrant (or valley) and crept up it. The ground was very rough and steep and there were horizontal ridges all the way up it. (In my view, these have been created by generation after generation of precariously feeding sheep and cattle: I cannot believe that even the most intrepid of ancient farmers could have actually made them with a plough.) From ridge to ridge we clambered upwards with a great deal of puffing and blowing. As we approached the fence at the top, we each grabbed a dog by the scruff of the neck, which added to the difficulty of the climb. At last we were there. Flat on our bellies we wormed our way (dog and all) up to the wire fence and surveyed the wide open spaces that stretched above us. Stephen pointed to the right. There, about seventy yards

away, sitting up on the skyline, was a hare. He man-
oeuvred Titus in front of him, one hand at his neck, the
other at the seat of his pants (the dog's). I did the same
with Rebecca. Both dogs were pointed in the direction of
the hare. They spent quite some time staring round in all
directions (I think they might have been a bit embarrassed by the rather odd way we were holding them).
Then Titus peered forward intently. He was looking in
the right direction, and he'd gone all tense. Stephen
nodded to me, and launched him into the open using an
action reminiscent of a straight drive at cricket. He made
off across the corn towards the hare. I launched Rebecca
and she followed him. The hare went away left-handed.
Titus turned after him; Rebecca followed. All three proceeded along the skyline, the hare cantering, Titus galloping, Rebecca strolling. The first two disappeared over
the top. Rebecca's head went up; she stopped, looked
about her, and then cantered back to where we stood.
She looked slightly confused. I wasn't quite sure what to
say, so I contented myself with a few encouraging
remarks and the odd friendly pat. After a bit, we walked
up to the gorse at the top. There was no sign of Titus. We
called and whistled, and had a cigarette. Ten minutes
later he came back to us. He was very tired, he lay down,
stretched out, and dug his nose into the turf. His heart
was pumping like a runaway steam-engine. We waited
till he had recovered and then carried on. We decided to
beat our way along the top and then work down and
back along the bottom. We started to walk along the
ridge picking our way between the gorse-thickets, and in
no time at all a hare got up under my feet and took off
across the corn on our right. I screamed and gave chase;
the dogs rapidly overtook me and went after him. This
time Rebecca went a bit faster and a bit farther. But even

so, before very long she gave up and came back. Once again Titus ran his heart out and returned slowly and in some distress. I remember I was beginning to worry about Rebecca: wouldn't it be awful, I kept thinking, if she was one of those dogs which simply would not hunt? And her with all that fine coursing blood in her veins! Titus, I reflected bitterly, was really showing her up; he wasn't meant to be a hunting dog at all, and hadn't had much practice, yet he was really trying to catch the blessed thing, while Rebecca just butterflied around behind him. However, I kept all this to myself and was nice to her.

Then we set off on the final stage of the operation. We retraced our steps to the brow of the hill and scanned the fields below. Stephen is not only beautifully put together (if on the fleshy side), he also sees like a hawk. Very soon he espied another hare, below us and to our right. We made our way along the top, selected a suitable fissure, valley, or re-entrant, clambered into it and made our descent (out of sight of the unsuspecting hare) to the edge of the field where he was. Thereupon the routine was as before, and the dogs were gripped, pointed, and launched. Actually there was a slight deviation; when Titus was launched, he didn't gallop, he trotted. This suggested to me that he hadn't seen the hare, so I hung on to Rebecca. Titus continued to trot in vaguely the right direction. The hare's ears twitched as he noticed the dog, and he loped off in the most casual manner. Titus saw him go, and broke into a canter. He, too, was unhurried. By now the hare was halfway across the field, and Titus trailed by some two hundred yards. Gradually he increased his pace. When the hare reached the lower fence, he was a hundred yards in arrears. Across the next field, still going directly away from us, he chopped the deficit in half. They crossed another fence, and the hare suddenly realised he had an enemy on his tail, and that he was far from the rugged heights where he had the advantage. He turned left-handed and piled on the pace. Titus turned and continued to close. The hare turned left again, in a gateway: they must have been half a mile away, yet we could see the earth fly as Titus skidded round after him. Now the hare was heading back towards the hills where refuge lay. Titus was close behind, but he couldn't make him turn; he bounced up the slope as straight as could be. After a bit the rigours of the day began to tell on the poor dog, and he started to lose ground. Meanwhile, up above, Stephen and I had been watching this fabulous chase with increasing delight. Luckily, Rebecca began to squirm with excitement, or I think I would have forgotten she was with us. Anyway, she did, and I came back down to earth. The hare was almost up to us: he was going to pass about twenty yards to our left. I climbed over the fence into the field, pointed Rebecca at him and let her go. She shot off like an arrow, and when he passed in front of her, she turned like the proverbial flash. Through the fence went the hare: through the fence went Rebecca—no shilly-shallying, no hesitation, no delay. Then they attacked that rough, steep, pitiless hillside. The hare bounded up, as to the manner born. Rebecca hurled herself in pursuit, head down, hind legs reaching ahead, and catapulting her body upwards. This was a different Rebecca: this was the real thing. It was as though she had suddenly remembered what life was all about; as though something had clicked into place in her brain as she watched that hare come racing back towards us.

We clambered back to the top. Some minutes later Rebecca came back: she was cooked; she was absolutely

exhausted; so was poor Titus. All they could do was to lie on the ground, and squirm and pant and wait for the violent rhythm of total effort to slow down and release them. We lavished praise and kind words and pats on them both. Titus especially deserved a medal. Then we went home to tea: it had been a lovely day, and boded well for the future. Nobody minded about not catching the hare; he had done a lovely job as a schoolmaster, and Rebecca, after two false starts, had passed her exam with flying colours. Anyway, he was a big, strong, downland hare. I don't think they'd have caught him in a month of Sundays; not on his home ground, anyway.

Soon afterwards Titus left the district. It was sad for Rebecca, who liked him very much, but probably it was best for him. For some time his owners had been aware that he wasn't too happy and that he wasn't leading the ideal life for a whippet. He had been a present and dogs make tricky presents. I mean, if you get given a perfectly monstrous china dish, you can always dispose of it in an attic; which you can't do with a dog. You have to make a bit of an effort; which is what Titus' people did. They made enquiries and tracked down a really good home for him and off he went.

Talking of morals (was one?), what about the morality of coursing hares? Myself, I take my dog out to catch a hare because I enjoy it. I also like eating hare and so does Rebecca. In addition, I know that hares do damage to crops and have to be killed. I also know that the normal way to get rid of hares is to shoot them. A hare shoot is not so much a sporting event as an annual chore—forty or so beaters beat them towards forty or so guns, and it is not unusual to kill two or three hundred in a day. In addition, a fair few are wounded and escape to die (or recover), in their own time. My sort of coursing (with only one or two dogs) is a very fair gamble for the hare; as often as not he gets away, with a grin on his face, slightly puffed, but otherwise unharmed. If he gets caught, he gets killed. Quickly.

7

What else happened during the spring of the year? One of my more vivid recollections concerns the Point-to-Points we attended. The first was the Old Wilts Hunt Point-to-Point. Since I had lived for several years in that part of the world, I went there confidently expecting to meet many old friends and enjoy a happy afternoon. Nor was I mistaken. Greetings flowed through the air like confetti, a variety of hands in all shapes and sizes were gripped and shaken. Glasses rose to the lips and returned to the bar with a rhythm so monotonous as to become almost hypnotic. Floating on a carpet of euphoria, I wandered (Rebecca at my side) towards the unsaddling enclosure. Behind it was the Clerk of the Course's Tent, the Gentleman Riders' Changing Tent, and the Lady Riders' Tent. In a word, this particular area belonged to Stewards, Owners, Jockeys, and various other categories of Very Important People. Suitably impressed, I kept my distance and gazed from afar. Then I saw a face I knew. Standing in the middle, wearing the badge of a steward (no less) was Mr Mills. I can't be sure (I have a wretched memory) that he was wearing a tweed hat, a tweed coat, tweed knickerbockers, and very exotic brown shooting socks, but, if not, I am sure it was something equally imposing. 'This is my moment,' said I to myself. I wheeled Rebecca up to him, introduced myself, introduced her, and waited in happy anticipation.

'Not very big, is she?' was his first observation. I flinched.

'Do you feed her?' he then said.

I looked around wildly for some place to hide. There were so many 'people', any of whom could well be overhearing every word.

'Has she got worms?' This was too much. Simmering with embarrassment, and not a little indignation, I took my leave and ran for cover.

The other one was at Larkhill. Rebecca spent the afternoon locked up in the Landrover. She played absolutely no part in the proceedings, which made it quite an unusual sort of day. (Incidentally, the tale that follows has nothing to do with dogs, and should be skipped if the reader isn't interested in horses.) I was having my one solitary ride of the season on a horse that I had qualified for a friend. (Oh! Those happy hunting days before this wretched dog came into my life to the exclusion of all else!) I thought I rode quite brilliantly that day, but all my friends were of the opinion that I should have been warned off. It was like this: there was a man who had for some time been interested in buying the horse in question. When first he saw it, he was rather rude about its lack of fitness, so I was fairly abrupt. (I didn't really want the horse to be sold.) I told him it would do this and then that, and then I said, '. . . it will run at Larkhill. It will go for two miles, and then it will be pulled up, and after that it will be Racing Fit!' To a great extent, naturally, I was guessing (one can never be certain in these matters), but I was irritated and I spoke with great conviction. Anyway, more by luck than good judgement, we got to Larkhill. The wretched man was there, clucking around like a pregnant hen. I swallowed several measures of liquid courage kindly provided by anxious friends, and we were off and running. Whereupon, the most extraordinary state of affairs became apparent: the horse was galloping and jumping like an electrified buck, instead of the sober old arthritic we knew him to be. Now, when you find yourself mounted on an electrified buck, and you only intend to go two miles, you have a distinct advantage over the opposition which rightly thinks that the race is a three-mile contest. The advantage has nothing to do with winning the race; it applies only to selling the horse. The horse, in these circumstances, can be made to look very good value indeed. You bound along and you make the others look very second-rate, and then, just as you begin to pay the price for excessive speed by getting tired, quick as a flash you pull up. This is what occurred. We bowled along in front, jumping every fence with unheard-of élan; then, when he began to labour a bit, and I could hear the rest of the field closing up, 'Whoa! My son,' said I, and we withdrew from the contest. At the thirteenth fence it was, the one in the dip, out of sight of the stands. Alas! When I got my breath back, I suddenly realised that an error had crept in. We weren't walking up a hill in the seclusion of Salisbury Plain, we were walking down one, in full view of the thousands who had gathered to bear witness. I had, as the saying goes, gone too far. I dismounted and led him back, yanking at his mouth (as gently as I could) to make him walk unevenly, and I rehearsed what I would say when they summoned me, and interrogated me, and tried to convict me of conduct unbecoming. 'Put his foot in a hole, Sir,' or 'Must have hit a nerve, Sir. Thought he'd broken his leg' (that one was very popular that year), or 'Tripped over a molehill. The state of the course is a disgrace.' (Perhaps that would be a bit strong.) We reached the crowd, and

51

no riot broke out; no official summons was issued; only the poor owner of the horse was almost too embarrassed to speak to me. Then I saw my prospective purchaser. I waited till I was in the cover of the parked cars and horse-boxes, and then I remounted and trotted up to where my trailer was, so that he could see for himself that the animal was 'sain et net' as the French have it. To cut a long story short, the animal was vetted on the Monday and swapped for a fairly hefty cheque on the Tuesday. A little bit of the currency found its way into my pocket, so the whole business was very satisfactory, especially as it gave me the opportunity to get away from that awful dog, if only for part of one afternoon.

8

Perhaps I should describe her, now that she is almost full size. When she approached you, you noticed first of all her flashy white legs and feet. Then you admired her flashy white waistcoat, neck and head; and you laughed at her odd brindled ear. When she got close to you, you were amazed and slightly alarmed by her very blue eyes. In shape, she was like a whippet, as far as her body was concerned, only an inch or so bigger, broader, and stronger all round. Good neck and shoulder muscles, and tremendous back legs; they bulged like weightlifters' biceps. Her head was odd, to say the least. It's a kind of pygmy bull-terrier head, very broad between the eyes, and then a long thin nose. More than anything else she looked like Anubis, the dog-faced Egyptian god. 'Not a poacher's dog' was how one expert described her. This is true because her white bits make her much too conspicuous.

T. H. White wrote a book called *The Once and Future King*, which became the film 'Camelot'. The film was a pathetic shadow of the book, and of the book itself the first part—there are three—was by far the best. In it, the hero (a boy called Wart, who becomes King Arthur in later life) is transformed—by Merlin—into a goose for a spell, then into a fish, then into a hawk—for educational purposes, naturally. Anyway, in this book there is a

description of an Arthurian pack of hounds, part of which goes something like this: 'And then there are the Alaunts, a cross between greyhound and bull-terrier, or even worse'; this has always been accepted by those who know her as a rather derogatory but fairly accurate description of Rebecca.

As for her being slightly larger than a whippet, I saw the living proof of this each week when I took her to visit Mrs Gordon. Instead of her dogs bullying Rebecca, now it was quite the other way around. As her size increased, so did her aggressive tendencies. Her favourite manoeuvre was galloping round (and through) the roses, heaving a whippet sideways with her shoulder and at the same time gripping its throat with her teeth. Not very good for the whippet, and tragic for the roses. Mrs Gordon, in spite of this, continued to laugh and to advise.

One other of Rebecca's natural attributes deserves to be mentioned: she is, for a dog, unusually talkative, and uniquely musical. I first noticed it in the evenings when I used to take her with me when I accompanied my master on his tour of the horses. This was a fairly lengthy process, and not laced with excitement. Rebecca would stand it for as long as she could; then she would register her protest with a long, high-pitched, growly sort of whine. Nothing of the sort had ever been heard in those circumstances before. The message was (as I soon discovered) 'I have had enough of this nonsense. Put me in the car or I will go on protesting, and the lads will go on grinning, and the master will eventually become irritated.' Naturally she got her own way. She has another signal, which starts off *basso profundo* and mounts swiftly to a *crescendo furioso*. This means "For heavens sake, let's go for a walk. Don't you realise that I go dotty if I don't get my exercise".

I suppose singing was a natural progression. To begin with, she used to accompany a certain type of hefty male voice, the sort one would find in Gilbert and Sullivan. Whenever she heard such a voice on the wireless, she would throw back her head and howl, and go on howling till it stopped. I thought it was a talent rather than a vice, and encouraged her. Then, one night, she decided to harmonise with Nana Mouskouri on the television. This I had to stop; I love my dog, but I prefer Miss Mouskouri on her own. Rebecca was furious. At first we thought that certain sounds hurt her ears, making her howl, but I don't believe that. One night I was in the kitchen at Framfield; a Joan Baez record was playing, very quietly, in the next room. We began to hear strange noises. We peered through the serving hatch; Rebecca stood in front of the fire quietly yodelling along with the record. She is not very musical by human standards, but compared with other dogs she has an enormous range and great powers of expression.

I suppose it must be obvious by now that my attitude to Rebecca was one of blind adoration, akin to that of a maudlin parent with an only child. Which being the case, I might as well be hung for a sheep as a lamb, and mention that she had yet another talent. One evening we were walking round the fox-covert at Darlingsford, when she suddenly froze and stared in front of her intently. Her near fore leg was raised off the ground and bent at the knee. She looked like a ballerina awaiting her cue. An interval elapsed of considerable length; long enough for anyone to flex their shooting muscles. (I don't shoot, but even I would have had the time to do the necessary flexing.) The tension was terrific and something had to give. There was a hysterical splutter from a tussock about ten yards away, and an unnerved partridge reached for the sky and beat a retreat. Rebecca watched it go, and then turned her head and looked at me, as much as to say 'How about that, then?'

9

It was about this time that I introduced her to my friend Barlow, who is tall and dark and generally admired by women. Not that he is just a pretty face; on the contrary, he is generously endowed with serpentine cunning. I realised this after studying his behaviour at parties for a number of years. It was (and no doubt still is) his practice to apply himself to the bottle, and to repeat the process frequently, until he was very drunk. Contemporaneously, he would adjust his behaviour from normal, to bad, to worse, to positively vile. He would shout and scream and belch and swear and roll on the ground and break things. When he achieved this positively vile' stage, he would maintain it until all his friends and acquaintances had noticed it, remarked on it, made loud censuring noises, and murmured their heartfelt sympathy to his wife. Anyway, when he has checked that everyone present has condemned him, out of hand, and preferably out loud, he moves on to the next stage. He adjusts his demeanour to 'perfectly civil' and throws himself, body and soul, into a frenzied round of primeval womanising—do not forget that he is strangely handsome, in a fairly ordinary sort of way. Young girls just out of school, and married women with devoted husbands, are his favourite targets. His technique never varies: a hangdog look and a shy smile, followed by

assiduous attention to unlighted cigarettes, empty glasses, chairs that require pulling back and doors that need opening; finally, a sudden lunge, a vigorous grapple, a speedy departure to the darkest corner of the dance floor, and Bob's your uncle. They love it. The clever part is that nobody says a word, not even the worried-sick mothers or the devoted husbands. All his potential critics have used up their ammunition blasting him for drunkenness; by the time they realise they have a real problem on their hands, their magazines are empty. He forces them to convict him on the minor charge, and thus renders himself free to get away with murder (or worse). What a mind! What profound understanding of human nature!

His house, flanked by a row of boxes, nestles in the shelter of a wood. After tea, he took me along the track that he had himself hewn with his own hands through the wood, to the paddock on the other side, that he, alone and unaided, had cleared, and mown, and fenced, and ditched.

'She's perfectly all right with sheep,' I said.

'You don't mind me asking? It's just that they're all in lamb. It would be rather a pity . . .'

There were about twenty of them. As sheep are wont to do, they moved in unison and, as it happened, they moved away from us. Which was fatal. If there's one thing that really turns Rebecca on, it's a mass departure. She blasted off like one of the better rockets, threaded her way through the fugitives, picked one to play with, segregated it from its fellows, and started chasing it round in circles. The others all disappeared at the top of the field, and when I say disappeared, I am picking my words. The top of the field is marked, properly enough, by a wire fence; beyond it is a precipice, otherwise known as a railway cutting. At the bottom there is a disused railway line. The sheep treated the fence with derisory contempt, and hurled themselves into the gaping void with an enthusiasm that would have commanded the respect of the Gadarene swine. We separated Rebecca from her new friend; the latter had adopted a prone posture and was pretending to be dead; Rebecca was lying beside her patiently awaiting the resumption of play. There was no time for recrimination; we hastened to the rescue of the others. It was hard work; they had patently fallen out of love with their paddock. A cutting has two sides and a bottom; when the sheep grew tired of being shepherded along one side, they bounced across to the other; when we covered both sides, they escaped along the bottom. Eventually they were restored to their place of origin. Still, it was too much to expect that all would instantly be forgiven and forgotten; the fact that they were all there, and seemed sound in wind and limb, was only half the battle. What about the great imponderable, the condition of their unborn offspring? The shepherd and his wife decided (and who can blame them?) to treat me and my dog as though multiple miscarriages were bound to occur.

Barlow's wife confided to me, at the top of her voice, that she thought Rebecca should be shot, and the sooner the better. Had they been my sheep—who knows—I might have agreed with her. I thought it wise not to accept a whisky and soda, even if it were offered. We took to the faithful mini and sped off. I suppose it took twenty-five minutes to get to Bobby's at South Hanney; hardly time enough to heave a sigh of relief and wipe the beads of sweat from the brow. We walked into the garden; I stopped to shut the gate; there was a roar of rage from behind me; I turned to find that Rebecca had assaulted one of Bobby's prize Muscovy ducks before his very eyes. I was sweating again. This time the whisky and soda was offered (purely as a way of getting the two of us out of the garden). I really enjoyed it; I needed it badly.

Which reminds me of Hettie, the legendary hen, who lived in the purlieus of the Casa Framfield, where I was wont to appear to partake of Sunday lunches. She was the golden, ruddy brown of a Henri Winterman packet of cigarillos. During the night she slept with the dogs in the kennel, where she was indisputably the boss; during the day the kennel was where she laid her eggs. Hettie was at liberty to wander where she pleased—all over the garden, and sometimes into the house. She had very little in common with other hens, and seldom sought their company. Apart from Henrietta, that is. Henrietta was another hen who preferred the company of men to that of fowl. Together, she and Hettie paraded up the drive, stalked across the lawn, and saluted their friends through the kitchen window. Whereas Hettie was on the plump

side, Henrietta was a tall, lean thoroughbred. Where Hettie had a short, low action (ignorant people might even describe it as a waddle), Henrietta lifted her knees, pointed her toes, and strutted. Hettie was golden brown, Henrietta palest beige, streaked with white, and her tail feathers were tall and dark. Altogether, they made a lovely couple, except that there were four of them, because Henrietta had two tiny yellow chicks that followed wherever she led.

Quod cum ita sit, as Cicero says, I was more than a little nervous about a confrontation between them and Rebecca, for Rebecca had given indications that she could not tell one hen from another (or from a hare, or from a horse, or from a sheep, or from a Muscovy duck). So when we next went for Sunday lunch, I got there early, and I was equipped with a long lead, consisting of three brown bootlaces and a length of string. I paid my respects to the company, harnessed Rebecca, and led her out on to the lawn. There we found Henrietta and her canary-coloured infants. I positioned myself in the centre of the lawn and paid out the line so as to give Rebecca every chance to feel free (or 'enough rope to hang herself', depending on how you looked at it). The little angel wandered around, and sniffed, and wagged her tail. When she came upon the chickens, she gazed at them with polite disinterest, stepped out of their way in the most courteous manner, and paid far more attention to a passing butterfly. Then she came up to me and intimated that she would quite like to exchange greetings with her doggy friends indoors. I was thoroughly elated.

In the middle of the afternoon, the tranquillity of the communal Sunday siesta was shattered. Two distraught children burst in and broke the news—before their very eyes Rebecca had murdered and devoured one of the chicks, and inflicted grievous bodily harm on the unfortunate mother. What a cow! What a scheming, untrustworthy, deceitful cow! I told her so, and many things besides, and she was punished savagely.

Much of the afternoon was spent finding the surviving chick, which had taken cover and was not to be seen. The cry of a chick is not very loud, and if you hear it, it is quite difficult to tell where it is coming from. Eventually we narrowed it down to a thorn bush. We surrounded it on three sides, the children and I, and peered inwards. After a bit, it cheeped and moved, and we saw it, but there was no way of actually getting at it. So we shepherded Henrietta in the direction of the bush; at last they spoke to each other, and soon after they were reunited. They looked a bit lonely as they paced off together. At times like that, I used to wonder what on earth was going to become of Rebecca; she seemed to be nothing but trouble . . . If she didn't improve, I reflected sadly as we drove home through the dusk, I won't be welcome anywhere in the South of England.

10

Her efforts in the hunting field during May and June were fairly pathetic. I came across an entry in my diary which read: 'May 6th; me screaming, waving, running after hare; Rebecca cantering beside me, gazing up in astonishment and sympathy.' This just about sums up the situation.

One evening towards the end of May, we went up to Slinford. I spent quite a long time crawling on my belly (Rebecca was on a lead), and eventually we found ourselves prone in the thick undergrowth by a wire fence that belonged to a field that was being cut for silage. Silage, being an agricultural thing, is a mystery to me; all I know is that they grow the grass, and then cut it, take it away, and feed it to the cattle in winter. The first stage of the cutting process consists of driving the cutter all the way round the outer edge of the field; as a result, the centre of the field is tall, uncut grass, which is green, framed all the way round by a strip of close-cropped grass, which is yellow (probably because the sun has not been able to get at it). This was the state of the field we were investigating, and into view hove a fine big hare, lolloping down the yellow strip without a care in the world, and with no idea that we were there. I held Rebecca and pointed her at it; she stared as though she were fascinated. When it was twenty yards away I gave her a push, and she lolloped off in quite the wrong direction and began chasing a bumble bee, which I suppose was what she was looking at all the time. I could have screamed; in fact I did. At this the hare turned on his heels and stumped off. At this point Rebecca condescended to notice it (or him), and went in pursuit. They made a stirring picture as they galloped away over the yellow turf in the evening sunlight, which did very little to relieve my disappointment, or Rebecca's exhaustion, which was all she got out of the episode.

I decided that we must go back to fundamentals; Rebecca must be encouraged to concentrate more, to go out looking for her prey, and not to daydream and vacillate. At the same time it would be wrong to involve her in anything too arduous. With these ends in view, we set out one day to hunt rabbits. We went up to a nature reserve on Manston downs (now that I come to think of it, hunting on a nature reserve was probably on the unethical side, unless rabbits are a pest anywhere). It is an extraordinary place, littered with enormous boulders, as if at some stage a nearby volcano had been liberally spraying the area with rocks. (In fact, my learned friends subsequently informed me that the Ice Age gathered up these rocks on its way down from the North Pole, and dropped them off as it retreated. They also informed me, rather contemptuously, that it was time I realised that volcanoes do not spray rocks all over the place. At the time, however, I was in love with the volcano theory, and I trod warily, in case it took it into its head to have another go.) There we were, and there were these hundreds of rocks, and above and below and around and upon them were thousands of rabbits. Even I could see them, but Rebecca simply refused to notice. I thought she might at least have indulged in a little bit of crouching, a little bit of creeping, a little bit of peering round corners, the occasional predatory dive. Not a bit of it. She trotted along, sticking out her toes, wagging her tail, nose in the air. I, on the other hand, moved silently and with extreme caution, as the situation demanded; when I spoke to her, I whispered, and when I reproved her, I did it *sotto voce*; she, naturally enough, took not the blindest bit of notice; she wasn't mad about doing what she was told at the best of times, and even at the best of times the only instructions she acknowledged were the maximum-volume ones. I lost my temper. Even then, I tried to be quiet about it, so as not to disturb the wretched rabbits. (Losing one's temper quietly places the system under an awful strain.) I needn't have worried about the rabbits; when I eventually lost control and started raving and jumping in the air, they thought it was the funniest thing they had seen for years; they crowded round to get a better look. Rebecca eventually did catch two of them (one had Myxomatosis), but her heart wasn't in it. I think she just did what she thought was enough to stop me making such an exhibition of myself.

The pattern of those early efforts is obvious: I was trying to push her too fast, too far, and too soon; she, being no fool, simply refused to be pressured. She had more important things to think about; apart from anything else, she was in love. The object of her affections was Billy, who belonged to Dinah's owner's brother (if you see what I mean). They met one Sunday, when all parties concerned foregathered for Sunday lunch. Billy was a couple of months older than her, a big handsome chestnut sort of a dog. When first they met, he was a bit leggy and awkward, and not the best of movers. Rebecca preferred not to notice this; as far as she was concerned it was love at first sight. He was the only dog in whose company she behaved even remotely like a lady; which was charming, but rather comical, because coyness was so out of character.

11

Rebecca's first hare didn't have all that much in common with Catherine of Aragon: for example, it was never heard to mutter anything memorable about the burghers of Calais, and it came to a violent end, whereas she was one of the few among Henry VIII's wives who were allowed to live unhappily ever after. Still they were both completely harmless, and extremely hard done by; and both are principally remembered as being the first of many. Henry married seven wives, and then gave up; Rebecca has been the undoing of ten hares and is still going strong. But then, marrying is harder work.

It was a hot day in July—July 6th to be precise. The heat was such that no-one would dream of wearing a jacket, not even if obliged to go and see the bank manager about the overdraft. That year there had been sunshine in May, and some people had jumped in and made their hay so fast the bales hardly touched the ground. Then it rained again, and they felt rather smug. Then the sun shone briefly: Other people cut their hay, but before they could turn, bale, stack, and store it, the rain returned and things looked black (and wet). The early birds felt even smugger. Then the sun shone again: the wet hay was salvaged, the rest was cut, and the whole of the operation progressed smoothly to a successful conclusion. Now the early birds felt pretty foolish, because they had cut rather prematurely, and everyone else had made better quality hay. Tricky business, farming. After one's dealt with the proper hay, one gets round to the less important stuff; like bad hay, and hay made simply to tidy up a piece of ground, and other people's paddocks, for one reason or another. Which was why the Darlingsford paddocks were being cut on July 6th, when I came back from the bank in my shirtsleeves. In the paddock across from the office, there was a square of standing grass which grew smaller every time the cutter went round it, slicing it down as it passed. The outside was all cut down and lying tidily in rows, except for one bit under the hedge where my three little jumps were. The man had left that bit out, because it was awkward to manoeuvre his machine between them. It occurred to me that it would be a bit awkward for me to manoeuvre a horse over them unless the grass was cut (however small an obstacle, it does help if one can see the bottom of it), so I thought I'd go across and ask him to have a go.

His name was Beadle; he was most obliging and said he would do what I asked. 'There's a leveret in there,' said he, nodding towards the standing grass, 'just right for your dog.'

'Which side?' I asked. He pointed to the top right-hand corner of the square. 'I should go over there,' he said, and sent us off to the bottom right-hand corner. When we were ready, he started to cut along the top. We waited at the corner. I held Rebecca pointing in the right direction, and we concentrated on the edge of the hay, where the tall grass ended and the open ground began. He had almost completed his cut along the top, when it bolted out in front of us, about thirty yards away. Rebecca saw it at once, and took off. It fled out into the open, turned, and scampered back into cover: Rebecca went in

after it. I could see the tall grass parting as it forced its way through, and, close behind, Rebecca leaping in the air to get a glimpse of her quarry, and then charging in pursuit. They did a half-circle and reappeared in the open. Two petrified leaps by the poor leveret, two bounds by Rebecca, and then she snapped it up and carried it off. I suppose my emotions were about on a par with those of Beethoven's mum, when first he took to the keyboard and the Austrian public gave him the big 'Jawohl'. I ran to where she had taken it; I smothered her in pats on the back; I took it off her and put it out of its misery; we showed it to Mr Beadle; he and I were unanimous that it was the finest bit of work we had seen for many a twelvemonth. Actually, it was a tiny little leveret, but one has to start somewhere, and lurchers can't be choosers. That is, some lurchers are so pursuit-minded that they have no option: when something moves, they chase. Rebecca was one of these, as I was beginning to discover. Within half an hour she gave me another indication of her character. I put the dead leveret in the boot of my car; Rebecca and I retired to the office to do some work. My concentration was broken by the sound of blood-curdling screams; I went out into the yard to find Rebecca firmly wedged by the neck under the wooden gates. She was trying to get to the boot of the car: such was her obsession.

At the end of July she caught another hare; once again, it was a young one, found in a paddock, and caught in a bush after the very shortest of chases. In between these minor victories, her hunting consisted of a series of defeats. Even when she put her mind to it, she was physically too immature to be a serious threat to an adult hare, and I was silly to encourage her. I noticed that after a hard course, she would take two or three days before she would once again be bucking and kicking and raring to go. (I found this particularly interesting in connection with racehorses. How does one know when a two-year-old has recovered from a race or a severe gallop? Bearing in mind the fact that a trainer probably only sees the horse for half an hour at morning exercise and for two minutes at evening stables; whereas a dog is generally with his master most of the day, and has all that time to show his condition.) To return to Rebecca: when she was worn out, or cold and wet, honey, eggs, and milk was her favourite tipple. I became a firm believer in eggs with everything; she looked pretty well most of the time (whatever Mr Mills cared to think), and she had four or five eggs a week.

My veterinary knowledge increased. I learned that permanganate of potash crystals dissolved in water, creating an exotic purple mixture, are good for hardening the feet; that butter, liberally smeared, is best for cuts, as the dog licks the butter, and 'lick' is the best possible antiseptic; that liniment rubbed between the toes because of suspected bruising can have alarming results: the patient is likely to start behaving like a mad thing, rolling on the ground, sliding on its back under furniture, biting itself, and uttering demented whines. However frightening, this is merely the sign that the liniment, too liberally applied to delicate skin, tingles and maybe stings.

As a dog-feeder, I discovered that cod-liver oil is good for the digestion (a fact which my years in the nursery had never taught me); it helps keep out the cold, and makes food taste irresistible (to dogs, that is); but too much of it can make the stomach work overtime, which is not necessarily a good thing. In the same role, I made friends with the butcher, who used to say, 'I know what you want. Five months old, isn't she? Leave it to me'. Then he'd flit along his row of meat trays, filling a polythene bag. From time to time he'd hold up some item and remind me that it had to be cooked. As a result, to this day I do not know the names of the types of meat Rebecca was brought up on; all I know is that it was good, and I can recognise the things that need cooking. I also learned that Carter Cana make by far the best dog biscuit. I used to nibble them while I was making her dinner; other varieties were reasonably tasty, but inclined to have the odd foreign body in among the biscuit (no doubt some very valuable nutritional additive, but quite revolting to find in one's mouth); Carter Cana, on the other hand, had the best taste and were biscuit through and through; in my opinion they add more to the pleasure of a glass of beer than any of your crisps or your salted peanuts. Strangely enough, I mentioned this to the man who used to sell them, and he confessed that he was quite partial to the odd handful himself. Maybe one day the makers will wake up to the quality of their goods, and they will appear in pubs and at cocktail parties for human consumption; in which case I would expect a small present.

Even in the sphere of philosophy, life with the dog was not without its lessons. For example, one morning I had a dispute with a horse; we neither of us liked the other, and in the end the argument was settled in his favour, because he flipped straight over backwards and crushed me something horrible. For three weeks I was a cripple. During this period I noticed how much better Rebecca handled misfortune than I did; when she felt sorry for herself, she just curled up and slept it off: whereas I couldn't stop moaning, complaining, and telling myself that things were bound to get worse before they got better. When she hurt a leg, she limped and carried on as best she could; when I was lame, I resigned from life completely until it mended. Oh, the pathos of discovering that even my blue-eyed dog was more of a man than I was!

12

August 12th was a bad day from the start, in fact from
three days before the start. That was when my master
told me that I was to go to Kempton to supervise the running of a horse called Otto, and that the diminutive
Smith was to ride. I had no grouse about the horse, or the
course, or the race, for the handicapper had been absurd-
ly lenient and, on paper, Otto should have been able to
win standing on his head. (Note for the attention of
horse-addicts only: handicappers, in these last golden
days before the computer take-over, vary from course to
course, and from meeting to meeting. The way to amass
an untold fortune is to run your handicap horses at the
meetings where the handicapper holds them in lowest
esteem, and therefore allots them the lightest weight to
carry. If, under such favourable conditions your horse
happens to lose, next time it may well carry even less
weight. At this point I am verging on the fraudulent, and
will end.) What I wasn't too happy about was the jockey.
In the Spring, had I not earnestly lectured this very
Smith on the importance of strengthening his puny body
if he was to have any chance of success in the saddle?
Had I not taken him out on the downs in the afternoon
and shown him exactly what he must do to improve himself? Had I not even taken a painful and undignified fall
in the course of my efforts on his behalf? All to no avail.

He would do nothing to help himself. Naturally when I saw that Otto was so leniently treated ('well in' or 'on a handy mark' are the expressions that spring to the lips), my reaction was along the lines of ' . . . Let's get the best jockey we can, and try to earn ourselves a few quid.' The difference being that when a horse like this—a colt, four years old, no longer a nervous infant—is ridden by a top jockey, he feels a man's strength on his back, he hears a man's voice telling him, in no uncertain terms, what is expected of him, and when he gets hit, it hurts. Whereas if it's a puny boy, the knees that grip him are like sparrows' wings, the voice is a plaintive squeak between gasps for air, and the rod that descends is more like a caress than a command.

We went in my own car, Rebecca and I, and the journey was murder. Have you ever tried driving to Sunbury on Thames in the heart of suburban Surrey, in a mini that overheats every five miles, on a day so hot that wiping one's brow is enough to make one sweat like a pig? Like a Bedouin, struggling from oasis to oasis on a hot day, I wandered from garage to garage plaintively bleating for water. After an age I discovered that a rubber pipe under the bonnet had an inch-long tear in it. Every time I poured the water in, the pipe poured it out again. We wound yards and yards of yellow insulating tape round it, and I found I could progress in fifteen-mile bounds. Having left Darlingsford at 11 a.m. we reached Kempton, fifty miles away, at 3.45 p.m. I left Rebecca in the car and went about my business. Otto was running in the 4.30; there were five runners. For most of the race he remained in fourth place; with two furlongs to go, he was pulled out to challenge; he got within a length and a half of the leader; then the ultimate pressure—the whip—was applied; he wriggled, shortened his stride, and I swear I heard him say 'Do that again; I like it.' When he returned to unsaddle—he had finished fourth, beaten by a head, half a length, and a head—he was yawning. His jockey, on the other hand, was in a state of coma induced by exhaustion and frustration. We dismissed him and he withdrew to change. Now I come to think of it, he did say something, when he managed to regain his faculties. He said 'Can I come back to the yard with you, instead of going in the horsebox?'

I had been expecting some vital intelligence pertaining to the race. I was puzzled. 'Why?' I asked.

'I want to go harvesting tonight. They'll go off without me if I'm back late.'

Harvesting. All he was thinking about was an evening's bale-carting. No wonder there is only one Lester Piggott. I told him about the state of my motor, and persuaded him that the horsebox was the better way.

'Embarrassing,' said the travelling lad, nodding towards the contented Otto. 'Everybody on this bloody course is sweating except him.'

Before going off to the stables with the horse, he asked me if I would call in at the weighing room to ensure that Smith took the colours away with him. Otherwise, he would have to come all the way back for them.

I did so, and then wended my way thankfully across the car park. The mini was there; the window was open; the dog was gone. It was like running into a brick wall on a dark night.

'Blue-eyed dog? Yeah, just seen 'im. 'E went that way' and off I went to the other end, calling at all the gates on the way, and always getting the same story. Rows and rows of cars, but no sign of Rebecca. At the far end is the railway station: hideous black trains kept thundering through, but nobody had seen her down there. I crossed the line and searched the open ground on the far side without success. When I got back the last race had been run, and dirty, grey hordes of people were filing out in all directions. Suddenly it was evening, and a nastier evening I cannot remember. I whistled, and a dog barked, and I ran. It was somebody else's Pekinese, in somebody else's car. I whistled till my mouth was dry and no whistle would come. Most of the exits are along one road, so I crossed it and combed the housing estates on the other side. When I got back, the car park was nearly empty. I went into the racecourse and looked around the woods that border the railway line; no luck. There was one more direction, down towards the bottom of the course. I searched the streets opposite the course without success, and then went across into the centre of the track. There I found a policeman exercising an Alsatian. No he hadn't seen her. Yes, he would keep an eye out for her. He pointed to the woods in the centre of the track.

'Dogs stray off into there and live wild for ages,' he said. 'Hundreds of acres of woodland. We once lost one of ours there; in the end we had to send in a bitch on heat; that fetched him.'

I went to the police station and reported her missing. 'Yes, blue eyes. No, no collar. No identity disc; nothing. But very blue eyes; you can't mistake her. Yes, I'd give a reward.'

I was tired. It was 7.30. I went back to the car and drove off. The vibration caused the windows to open slightly; it had been doing this for months, ever since the catch stopped working. I now realised what had happened and I could just see her, sitting on my seat with her nose through the gap, working it open. Then a scramble up, and a jump down, and then what? There was a cold draught. I slammed the window shut. I was meant to call in at Framfield for supper so I headed that way. When I was nearly there, at the top of the village in fact, I turned off and pushed on to the cottage. I didn't feel in the mood for supper and company.

Thursday was the day of the frog-in-the-throat, and no mistake. It seemed that every time I wanted to speak it would leap up into my mouth, and I would have to gulp and swallow before I could get the words out.

I sent a telegram to Battersea Dogs Home, because the Sunbury police had told me that all strays from their area were likely to end up there. Their phone number is ex-directory; if it weren't, they'd be snowed up by calls from my type of lunatic.

'. . . blue-eyed (gulp) whippet-type bitch (gulp) stop. Brindle body (gulp) white head and legs (gulp gulp) . . .' It was murder. Of course, the secretary heard me phoning the telegram, and she was upset, and sympathetic, which made it even more difficult. I didn't know where to look, and I had to be careful choosing my words when I spoke to her, and I always seemed to be out of breath and liable to finish every sentence with a gasping rush.

There was plenty of work to do in the office, and I got through the day all right, by just concentrating on what I was doing and not thinking about dogs. I immersed myself in entries and forfeits and declarations and withdrawals. When I had exhausted that lot I turned to leaking roofs, overflowing cess-pits, and an outbreak of gastric flu among the stablemen. Nobody else noticed that she wasn't there, so that was all right. By evening I felt I had adjusted to the situation and could put up with it.

At six o'clock I went into the hostel to put away the office key. 'Here you are,' said Mrs Morgan, and handed me a little parcel of bones for Rebecca, wrapped in greaseproof paper; she had done the same twice a week since the beginning.

'I've lost her,' I said. She really liked Rebecca, and she is the kindest woman I have ever met, and her face reflects her character. If I had known she really didn't care at all, or if she hadn't shown it so clearly, it would have been much easier. As it was, I had a very traumatic five minutes telling her all about it. She was so upset and so kind that I felt awful. My determination to be firm with myself and 'indifferent' about what had happened simply melted away. When I left her I thought I was the saddest man in the world.

Which was not the ideal state of mind for meeting Paul, who popped in to the cottage unexpectedly that evening, where I was rather miserably minding my own business. Paul was strong and tough; he shrugged off his own misfortunes, and laughed at other people's; and he didn't much like dogs. He used to pick Rebecca up and bite her leg until she squealed. I braced myself against the moment when he would turn the whole thing into a joke. But he didn't. He was kind, he was gentle, he was extra diplomatic—which made it much, much worse.

'Come to supper. No good being on your own.'

'Thanks very much, but I couldn't face the sympathy.' I couldn't even face him; whenever I had to say something, I seemed to have to go and look out of the window.

The same old arguments kept running through my mind, again and again, and again. Why hadn't I organised a proper place to leave her while I went racing? I had had her long enough to work something out, if I hadn't been so idle. Only an idiot takes a dog racing in a mini on a boiling hot day. Why did I have a car with broken window-catches? I wasn't rich, but I was rich enough to get my windows mended, especially if I was going to keep my dog in the car. Why had I undertaken to keep a dog at all, when I was obviously in no position to do so? What right had I to step in and adopt the poor thing (casually, carelessly, without a thought for the responsibilities involved), when she could have gone to some far better home and lived happily ever after?

The cottage was very quiet without her.

13

Friday morning found me feeling rather like Keats's knight-at-arms, 'alone and palely loitering'. ('The sedge has withered on the lake, and no birds sing.') I am sure he didn't find life any grimmer than I did. The only solution was to go to the office and work like a demon. Luckily it was wages day, which was a good thing, because on wages day I find it very difficult to think of anything other than wages: I am always slightly haunted by the possibility that I may be robbed on the way back from the bank, or that some miscalculation may result in there being less than enough money and that one will have to explain it to a mob of rioting unpaid lads. So I tend to concentrate rather hard, and to heave a sigh of relief when the packets have been filled and the money has balanced. Which, thank God, is what happened this Friday. Then I reached for the phone, rang the Sunbury police, put the burning question and got the inevitable reply; they had no news for me. Back to square one, only now I had no pressure of work to keep me distracted. I sat and brooded until I got fed up with sitting and brooding, and then I wandered up to the top yard on some pretext or other. Maybe I had something to do up there; I don't remember: I know it was nice to get out of that dark little office into the sunshine. The paddocks were bright green, the birds were singing, and the lads at the top, as always, were good for a laugh and a friendly gossip, which was what I needed.

When I got back, the secretary looked excited. She said 'You're to ring the Sunbury police. They were just on the line. I looked for you.'

'I was up at the top,' I said. I rang them.

'Just after we put the phone down to you,' the voice said, 'this woman rang. Says she's got a blue-eyed whippet. Hold on and I'll give you her name and address. Yes, she's on the phone: I'll give you her number.'

She was called Mrs Marler; I had a long chat with her; the beginning was liberally sprinkled with lots of 'I can't believe it', the middle contained several versions of 'Thank you so much' and 'Aren't I the luckiest?', and I remember it ended with 'Don't you let her out of your sight, please. See you about three o'clock'. Then the phone was replaced, and joy abounded in the office.

There followed the agonies of the frustration of delay; I decided to take the master's van, as I didn't fancy the mini's chances. I packed up the office and went round to the garage—the master's van was missing. Jeff's van was there, and I was told that he had taken the master's to the garage for minor repairs and would be back shortly. Shortly lasted three-quarters of an hour, during which I paced between the garage and the office, or stood by the gate staring at the traffic. When he still didn't come, I left him a note of explanation, and took his van. The journey went well—I had to keep on reminding myself not to go too fast—until I got somewhere near Virginia Water. There a lorry had decided to crash and spread itself right the way across the road. As a result, there followed an agonisingly slow detour round backstreets for about six miles; it seemed to take all day. Eventually I found myself in familiar surroundings. I drove past the railway station, past the carpark entrances, past the spot where I had met the policeman with the Alsatian, and on beyond the point where I had ended my search. Half a mile further I stopped and got directions to the housing estate where Mrs Marler lived. It turned out to be only a little further on. I parked the van and found the house on foot. Mrs Marler was standing in her garden looking out for me.

We went into an L-shaped room. I couldn't see anything in front of me, so I peered round the corner. Rebecca was lying on a sofa. She looked at me, then lifted her head and looked again. Then she heaved herself up, flopped down on to the floor and walked across; every step seemed to be a terrible effort. Then she began to wag all over, not just her tail but her whole body. She threw herself at me, and I lifted her up and held her in my arms. When I put her down, she gave a sigh, walked slowly back to the sofa, pulled herself up and stretched out. She didn't move again till it was time to go.

Mr and Mrs Marler were delightful people. They had two dogs of their own, and the awful thing is that I can't remember what sort of dogs they were; I did get the impression that they were very attached to them. I suspect that perhaps they were the biggest thing in their lives, that they got all the love and attention that he used to give to his business (he was now retired), and that she used to give to her children (who were now grown-up and had families of their own). Which was a lucky thing for Rebecca and me. They gave me a glass of beer, and told me the tale which was as follows: on the Wednesday night, while walking their dogs, they had come across this extraordinary blue-eyed creature, which was friendly towards the dogs but wouldn't have anything to do with the humans. On Thursday morning she was still around, and they still couldn't get near her. Thursday night, she had sat on their doorstep and howled, but when they opened the door, she took off. On Friday morning, there she was again. Mrs Marler decided it was time to take action, so she produced a tin of dog-food and enticed her into the house. She ate, bedded down on the sofa, and went to sleep. Mrs Marler rang a friend (a vet, I think she said), and asked what she should do next; she was advised to inform the police, which is where I came into the picture.

They really liked Rebecca; they told me that they had wanted to keep her; that they had hoped she wouldn't be claimed; and that if she hadn't made it obvious that she recognised (and quite liked) me, they wouldn't have let her go. They wouldn't accept any sort of reward.

I drank the beer, and told them all about Rebecca, and asked them to come and visit us. Then it was time to leave. It was about a hundred yards to the car. Halfway, Rebecca had to stop and lie down and have a rest; I never saw such an exhausted animal.

On Sunday—very bright but not too early—we drank a lot of Pimms with our friends in Stephen's garden. He insisted it was a Welcome Home party for Rebecca; I can think of no better excuse. The fact that the invitations were issued several weeks before is neither here nor there. Rebecca enjoyed it; she made the acquaintance of Maxwell, a three-months-old, black, very floppy, Labrador, Stephen's latest acquisition.

During the week that followed her return, she was very quiet. She would have the occasional jump and kick, but they were always followed by a lie-down in the sun, which was quite out of character. My zoologist friend Geoffrey told me this was the result not just of physical hardship but of nervous exhaustion as well. On Tuesday

28th, thirteen days after I lost her, and eleven after I got her back, I wrote in my diary: 'It's happened; suddenly all day long she's bouncing, chasing, jumping up, racing off, wrestling with flies on the window, catching hold of shadows in the barley.'

I had been very lucky. The odds against finding any lost dog must be considerable; those against finding one lost fifty miles from home even greater; greater still when the dog carries no form of identification (I went and ordered a collar, with her name and address on, the very next day). Besides which, the chances of a dog surviving thirty-six hours on the streets of Sunbury without being run over must be pretty slim. Altogether, very lucky indeed; I resolved not to leave so much to Providence in the future.

14

The horse side of the story—the next page or so contain nothing but horse gossip and are not compulsory reading —was a miserable failure, although immediately after the race it seemed full of promising possibilities. The facts were as follows: Otto had been allotted eight stone in the Kempton race; the apprentice allowance reduced this to 7st. 7lb. He finished fourth. The interesting part is that he was only beaten a length and a half or there-abouts; if he had finished last, beaten fifty lengths, the reaction of the average handicapper would be, 'This can't be his real form; take no notice of it; continue to allot him 8st. in handicaps.' However, in this case the horse was right up there in the forefront of the battle, and apparently doing his best to win. The handicapper might well have thumbed through the appropriate Racing Calendar to see if he could find some notice to the effect that the Kempton Stewards had deported Smith for life, for blatant lack of effort in the race in question. Not find-ing any such thing, he might well have said something like 'By Jove! By Golly! By Jingo! If the hawk-eyed stew-ards found no fault with the horse or the jockey, they must indeed have been doing their damndest; yet, with a paltry 7st. 7lb. on his back, he could do no better than finish fourth; perhaps I've overrated him; (anyone can make a mistake; give the fellow a fair crack of the whip)

maybe I should take a few more pounds off his back.'
Which, believe it or not, is what happened; two weeks
later a handicap appeared, compiled by the man who
had 'done' the Kempton race, in which Otto had such a
weight advantage over his rivals, that he could have
fallen down, got up, bitten the starter's assistant, and
still won (to misquote Edgar Wallace). Racing villains
have been shot time and time again for trying to do what
we had accomplished. We, I suppose, were entitled to get
off fairly lightly on the grounds of diminished respon-
sibility; nobody concerned actually knew what was happening until it was done. I must admit that when I
scrutinised the race in question my soul was full to burst-
ing with unholy glee; the habits of my sinful youth die
hard, and I tend to get disgustingly excited by anything
that suggests a 'steal'. Sad to relate, the story has anything but a joyful ending. Triumphantly I waved the
Calendar under the nose of my master. I said 'Look at
that!'—which was where I made my big mistake. It is a
fact of life that trainers are contrary beasts (why this
should be, I do not know, but it is indisputable); if you
want them to do something with one of their horses,
always suggest the opposite. If you want a trainer to run
a horse in a certain race, by all means leave the Racing
Calendar under his pillow, or in his handkerchief
drawer, or nailed to the starting gate out on the downs
(Most odd! I can't think how it got there); but never,
never actually tell him what he should do. He will inevi-
tably find a good reason to run the horse somewhere else,
where it has no chance, and gets beat. Which is what
happened in this case. Still, one learns by one's mistakes.

Which reminds me of Smith. Soon afterwards he announced that he would like to be released from his
apprenticeship, in order to take up some other form of

occupation. Maybe he was wise. Perhaps he realised there was no point in continuing half-heartedly in a career that demands total involvement.

15

On the last Sunday in August (and the eighth after Trinity) I attended my once-yearly cricket game. In a normal year I would have been the sort of player who bats number eleven and is never asked to bowl, but none the less a player. This year, owing to another disagreement with a horse, I was a rather lame spectator. This particular annual gathering is more than just a game of cricket, as most of the participants have a variety of interests besides bat and pad. There's beer-drinking for the beer-drinkers; gin-drinking for the gin-drinkers; racing reminiscences for those who are that way inclined; a lot of meaningful talk about the harvest; and watching courting couples on the hills above the ground through binoculars for those with binoculars. Rebecca was very interested in all that was going on, particularly in Billy, who was there on account of the fact that his master plays a mean game of cricket. Together they galloped from group to group making certain that everyone was enjoying themselves; twice they held up the game by coursing the ball; this didn't worry me too much, as by now Rebecca's eccentricity was well known and generally accepted; however Billy's owner (who is very proper in all respects) was somewhat put out that his dog was being, as he put it, 'led astray'. After a while I noticed that she was paying less attention to Billy, and more and more to a certain car in the row of cars drawn up along the boundary. I wandered over to investigate and found myself peering through the window at a whippet, which was in a state of great excitement. Then it dawned on me —it was Titus. I ferreted out his connections, and arranged his release, and there were scenes of intense rejoicing so that the game was held up again.

From the way they behaved, I could imagine a conversation that went something like this:

'Titus, Oh Titus, how awfully, spiffingly nice to see you. I bet you don't remember me.'

'My dear young lady, of course I do. Aren't you the delightful Rebecca Simpson?'

'You do remember me!'

'And didn't you have a day's hunting with us at Slinford before I moved to this part of the world?'

'I'm afraid I was awfully bad; I didn't have much of a clue.'

'Nonsense, dear girl, you were excellent. It was your first day, wasn't it?'

'Yes it was, and I really was awfully spastic.'

'Fiddlesticks, my dear, you soon got the hang of it; I remember it well; we didn't kill, but we finished off with a tremendous run, and you were bang up in front. I can see it now.'

'You're much too kind, Titus. I say, do let's go off and rag Billy; he's being awfully huffy about something, I can't think why.'

The story of how he happened to be there was a classic example of the smallness of the world. Soon after I met Paul (Titus's ex-owner), I introduced him to Mrs Gordon. When Paul decided to part with Titus, naturally he contacted her, as she is the undisputed queen of the whippet world. She has a son who went to a school where there was a master who was overheard bewailing the fact that he hadn't got a dog. Son reported back to mother. Mother sent messages to master. Master and dog were invited to meet each other at the Gordon house; the meeting was a success, so mother gave her blessing to the union, and the deal was done. Finally, to complete the circle, I had been acquainted with the master for several years, because he was the highly efficient wicket-keeper in my once-a-year game. Titus looked well and happy; his connections assured me that they loved him dearly; their side won the game.

16

September was the month of good resolutions, with which, I understand, the road to hell is paved. The first of these was to the effect that Rebecca should not be allowed to hunt until she was a bit older. The plan was that she should be kept on a lead when we went on the downs, that whenever possible we should take our exercise where no hares dwelt, that she should be fed with much nourishing food, and encouraged to take long naps regularly. Let it be admitted here and now that there was, from the start, not the remotest possibility of this plan ever succeeding. First of all, she had for months been encouraged to gallop, and now really needed that sort of exercise. Secondly, she had been encouraged (or at least allowed) to chase anything that moved, and was not likely to change that attitude in a hurry. Thirdly, it was madness to feed her up in these circumstances, as it only made her fresher and keener.

Anyway, I tried. Limping horribly, I would take her out on the end of a lead. As soon as she saw open country, she would start rearing and pawing the air, heaving, straining, and leaping, to the accompaniment of hideous choking noises from her throat. The whole performance was a considerable ordeal, not least for me. While I tried to restrain her, my arms and shoulders

were under considerable pressure, and when she suc-
ceeded in forcing me to go faster, my back and legs did
not like it at all (I was still a mass of bruises at the time).
I dreamed up an alternative; I decided to keep her
indoors as much as possible. Alas, this was no better, for
Rebecca insisted on her regular exercise; 'indoors' made
no difference to her. She knocked over everything that
could be knocked over. She chewed everything that could
be chewed. Her favourite thing was cornflakes, which
could be knocked over first and chewed afterwards. She
was also quite sure that she could help me back to perfect
health, so whenever she found me doing something, she
would feel obliged to join in. This was not a good thing:
sweeping the floor, for example, is not my idea of fun at
the best of times, let alone when one is the worse for
bruises. However, it is twenty times more tedious when a
demented dog is convinced that the head of the broom is
'the enemy', to be harried with tooth and nail, and that
the accumulated sweepings are treasures to be snatched
up, carried off, and hidden in a variety of convenient corners. If she found me sitting quietly minding my own
business, or reading a paper, or just staring into space
(which is a thing that the poet recommends having
plenty of time for), she, being totally ignorant of any sort
of poetry, would throw herself upon me and demand a
wrestling match.

I thought again. Very well, I decided, out we will go;
and we will dispense with the lead. But, we will only go
to those places where we positively know there are no
hares. Once again I never had a chance. When you want
a hare, you can't find one; but when you really don't
want one—everywhere you look, hares.

Like the afternoon that I decided to drive out to in-
spect the new track that was being rotovated out of virgin

downland (as an extra trotting-ground for the horses in the winter). It just so happened that before we reached the spot, the mini overheated (not for the first time). Lights started flashing, dials registered 'dangerous', and ominous wisps of steam drifted heavenward. So we walked the last bit of the way, Rebecca and I, and we had our chat with the rotovator. We walked back to the car. Just before we reached it, up got a hare and a chase ensued that involved five or six turns. At times Rebecca was no more than a foot from success, but each time a well-judged turn sent her sprawling and lost her valuable lengths. Each turn took the hare nearer and nearer to the rough ground. Finally he reached it, disappeared into the wilderness, and Rebecca was forced to give up. The point is, we weren't looking for a hare at all; it was the last thing on earth we wanted to see (speaking for myself, that is). The same thing happened on the 7th of September, and on the 9th, and on the 11th, and each time the hare was unwanted, unexpected, uninvited, and unwilling to be caught.

On the 16th we were, I admit, on the downs, and she was not, I admit, on a lead. But we weren't looking for any sort of trouble, we just wanted to have another look at my track. My diary says: 'Tonight we went looking at my track. We had just got round to noticing that the downs, on a fine evening, are among nature's best bits of work, when a hare got up, and she started hunting. Through the rough, onto gallops, out of sight, and back again. Round our front, round again, and back into rough. I thought that was the end. Seconds later saw flash on horizon. Seconds after that heard squealing. Advanced. Halfway up hill, there she was, sitting over dead hare. What a beauty!' Her first proper course, her first victory; I suppose it deserved something better than the account I jotted down at the time. Actually, I don't mind too much, because I was a spectator of the event, and my diary, however terse and badly written, triggers my memory and enables me to see it all again. However, the reader is not in the same happy position, so maybe I should describe the incident at greater length. The sun was just setting behind the hill; the sky was clear, and if one looked West one was blinded by a barrage of cold, white light. All other directions were full of undulating downs, tidy gallops, and long shadows. Rebecca found this hare in the rough; she started buzzing around with her nose down, and I watched her. I thought it was just another fascinating smell that had got her going. Then she started motoring rather faster than is normal with fascinating smells, and indulging in ecstatic jumps to look over the top of the tall undergrowth. All this was going on on my sunny side, so I was having to shade my eyes to see anything at all. Then she proceeded out of the sun, and I could see. She headed towards the gallops. Something moved in the corner of my vision; I focused on it, and it was a hare that appeared out of the rough. Rebecca followed and the two of them disappeared over the side of the hill. Silence all around, while I stood and wondered whether they would turn left and re-appear up the hill, or right and re-appear down in the valley. This was a left-handed hare; they circled back through the point where it all started, round in front of me again, and headed off as though to disappear once again. However, this didn't happen, because the hare turned sharp left before the descent began, and headed straight up the hill, through very rough terrain, and what is more, steering due West, which was directly into the glare of the sun. I became resigned to the fact that the odds were heavily against Rebecca and that success was unlikely. Making some effort to shield my eyes and peer ahead, I trotted slowly after them. The 'flash' on the horizon obviously wasn't a flash; the horizon was one big glowing flash already; I suppose what I really saw was something black and moving. 'It's still happening,' I said to myself, and pressed on. Awfully uncomfortable, trying to run uphill (or downhill for that matter) with one hand shielding the eyes. About the squealing I have little to say; one hears it, and it means something. It makes one run faster, but it is not very pleasant. I changed direction and made for the source of the sound. There she was, very blown, and really rather pleased with herself, which she had every right to be. I, naturally, was beside myself with joy. January, February, March, April, May, June, July, August—quite a long time, not all of it pleasant, not all of it easy; but now at last the real business was beginning, and the omens looked propitious.

I tried not to let success go to either of our heads; I did my best to avoid hares, and constantly reminded myself (and Rebecca) that she had her whole life in front of her, that there was every good reason to take things slowly for the time being. It wasn't easy; temptation seemed to lurk round every corner; if one dropped one's guard for just a second, something awful happened. For example, once we took a stroll on the downs after lunch. (Rebecca was on a lead.) As luck would have it, I began to feel fearfully drowsy (it was that sort of afternoon), and there was this particularly inviting rock, against which it seemed imperative that I rest my back. One simply cannot go to sleep with a dog on a lead (it would be most improper); I released her, and dozed off. I was awoken by the sound of plaintive squeaking and laboured gasping: the squeaking came from a hare, the gasping from Rebecca (when you're out of breath, and your mouth is full of hare, you gasp). If anyone had been watching, it must have been a bit comical: the life-and-death struggle all over the downs, the capture, and then the unfortunate quarry being lugged off and laid at the feet of the doting master who has slept his way through the whole drama. At the time I didn't think about the comic side; I was berating myself for dereliction of duty. I told my worries to my friend Stephen. 'I can't stop her,' I complained. 'Every bloody day some stinking hare has to get in her way. The strain could damage her heart; for all I know the harm may already have been done.' 'What we need,' said Stephen without hesitation (Stephen is mentally as agile as a monkey), 'What we need is Titus and a shotgun. We find a hare, Titus is sent in pursuit, Rebecca is restrained; Titus does all the donkey work; Rebecca can be loosed off just in time for the kill. If the hare won't be reasonable, I'll 'av at 'im with the shotgun.' For all I know it might well have been the answer. We never got round to trying it, because at this point I became involved in the second of my September resolutions—canine reinforcements.

17

After considerable thought I decided that it was no use fighting against *force majeure* (whatever that means). In a word, if hares insisted on provoking her, let her hunt them, *but* let her have a mate, companion or partner to share the load. What is hard work for one dog on its own, becomes easy when there are two dogs together. When the hare turns, it may well send the first dog sprawling; but it is quite likely to find itself heading 'into the jaws of death' or at least into the mouth of the second dog. Again, when a hare turns, the first dog may well have to turn after it, while the second could easily be in a position to cut the corner and close on his unsuspecting quarry from an unexpected angle. I am sure there are many other ways in which duplicity of dogs is an advantage; in time I suppose I will get to know them all. At that stage the two I have mentioned were enough to send me scurrying round looking for a little helper.

As was my custom, I consulted Mrs Gordon. As was her custom, she produced the perfect answer instantly. She shuffled through her pack of jokers (whippets, actually); rejected A, B, and C because they were too young; also D, E, and F because they were too pretty, too valuable, and had numerous prizes to prove it; settled for G and H. G and H were experienced coursers who had caught no end of hares, and rabbits in such numbers that it was lucky for rabbits that they breed as they do. We arranged that I should name the day; if it suited her, we would meet at a meeting-place, and proceed to scour the downs with three dogs.

'How about Wednesday?' said I, when I rang on Monday.

'Wednesday will do well,' she replied. 'I think I'll bring all my dogs.'

A twinge of misgiving stirred me. 'I thought you only

wanted to bring two,' I said.

'All of them,' she persisted.

'There are sheep in the neighbourhood,' said I.

'My dogs don't chase sheep,' said she haughtily.

I stifled further objections. Who was I to question her judgement? She was the expert who had steered me through all the pitfalls of Rebecca's childhood. If she chose to appear with a thousand dogs, I wasn't entitled to raise even an eyebrow, let alone a protest. We agreed to meet at the lay-by on the Galton road at 6 p.m. on the Wednesday evening.

It was hardly a success. I will let my diary describe it for me: "What an 'orrible experiment. 'It was a dark, windy, cloud-swept evening. (I suppose I meant "dark, cloudy, wind-swept evening". I wrote my account the same night; I was too irritated to write good English.) Mrs Gordon arrived, plus six yapping twits of dogs. We walked a long way and saw no hares and it began to get dark. Then I said "Where's Rebecca?" and after a pause she said "There she is. At the top of the hill. Can't you see her? You must be blind. She's after a hare. Isn't she good? She's turning it; she's turning it; she's turning *with* it. Isn't she good?" Meanwhile her bloody dogs who were at liberty to wander wherever they wanted throughout a vast tract of Wiltshire downland were fiddling about at our heels, yapping contentedly, swapping gossip among themselves, for all the world like a lot of old crones. Eventually Rebecca came back exhausted. Supper chez Gordon: snails and boeuf stroganoff; not bad. Home.'

I think it was at this point that I began to see the writing on the wall as far as Mrs Gordon was concerned. Nothing dramatic, mind you; I continued to admire her as much as ever. However as I read through my diary I detect the beginning of an independent attitude to the problems of a dog's life, and I suspect that something had undermined my faith in that particular oracle; it could well have been that ill-fated cloud-swept Wednesday evening. Not that I wasn't eternally grateful for the snails etc.

18

The Lambourn lurcher show (the next major event) was intended to be a purely parochial happening. It was designed to provide a certain amount of amusement for the local dog-owners (Lambourn boasts more weird dogs than the average village), entertainment for the natives, and money for a deserving charity, the name of which escapes me. As things turned out, it caused a considerable stir in lurching circles throughout England, and even as far as Scotland. Lurchers and their humans congregated from all points of the compass in great numbers. A good many of the dogs, it is true, were only lurchers in so far as no other word would define them; but the majority were the genuine article, and were an impressive indication of the widespread interest that exists in the type.

I, naturally, was full of widespread interest as I drove, that Sunday morning, into the field that was the scene of operations. On the near side were two or three rows of parked cars. Along the middle a rough course had been marked out for the racing, which was to be the finale of the proceedings. On the far side there was a ring for the various classes, and an obstacle course for testing the suppleness of dogs and masters. When I arrived and parked, I couldn't see the layout of the field; I discovered it all later by walking around and looking; I couldn't see because of the vast number of people and dogs wandering about enjoying the weather and exchanging greetings. I found that, as I had expected, lurchers come in all shapes and sizes; I made the new discovery that their owners are no less variegated. There were horsey folk dressed as though they had either just come off the gallops, or just emerged from the muckheap, or were just about to launch themselves into the paddock at Ascot. There were doggy folk kitted out for Crufts, and doggy folk kitted out for a wet afternoon at Wandsworth Greyhound Stadium (with the possibility that the three dog in the fourth was a lay-down certainty). There were lots of gypsies. They moved around in little self-contained groups, didn't make a lot of noise, and took in everything with keen professional eyes. The same applied to their dogs. There were farming folk who were only there for the beer, and city folk celebrating the weekly escape from the cities. I don't think I have ever seen so many children at a sporting event, but then I suppose children and dogs are inextricably involved with each other. Sometimes children were in charge of dogs, sometimes vice versa, and the situation fluctuated from extreme to extreme, and from moment to moment.

Mrs Gordon stood out like a veritable Maypole with six whippets dancing round her on leads. When she wasn't careful—and conversation often got the better of concentration—they tied her up in a knot and she had to be unravelled and rescued.

Billy was two cars away from us. Lots of:

'How awfully nice to see you.'

'Jolly nice to see you too. This your first show?'

'Yes, it is actually. What are you going in for?'

'My master thinks I might win the Smooth Dogs. Of course, I'm still eligible for the Puppies, though you'd hardly think it.'

'I'm sure you'll win the Smooth Dogs. I'm in the Smooth Bitches; most of them are much bigger than me: It hardly seems fair. Bet they couldn't catch a snail, silly bitches.' And so on. On the other side of Billy was Dinah, looking very distinguished and grey-maned. The car next to us belonged to a very attractive dog, a little bit bigger than Rebecca. When she saw him, she went potty: sort of: 'Is it ? Is it? Can it be? Are my eyes playing tricks?

'Lord above, it jolly well is! How are you, how are you? It's been such a long time. Do you remember me? I'm little Rebecca.'

It turned out that he was none other than her long-lost brother Nomad, whom she hadn't seen since she was seven weeks old; they were ecstatic about each other. He is about two inches taller than her, with none of her bull-terrier features; in fact, he has a very handsome long-dog head (I would prefer that Rebecca should remain in ig-norance of the opinion I have just expressed). Like her, he is brindle, but instead of her sober brown brindle, his is an exotic apricot blend. His eyes are deep brown, and altogether he is a most taking creature; to prove it, he went and won the Smooth Dogs class, beating Billy, but that didn't happen till later. At the time, he and his sister were engrossed in a series of energetic stand-up how-d'you-dos: an embrace that was a mixture between a double hug round the neck and two simultaneous pats on the back, possibly something like a meeting between two friendly French wrestlers. I was introduced to Nomad's owner: introductions, greetings, compliments, insults, and odious comparisons were exchanged like machine-gun fire. (It is strange but true that when two perfect strangers own related dogs, they immediately start to behave with a familiarity and warmth that would normally, among the English, take years to develop. This might be a bad thing if they later discovered that they loathed each other. However that wasn't our problem: at the time we found each other charming, and as we haven't met since, there has been no deterioration in the relationship.)

At about this point, Rebecca got loose and galloped off. ('Dogs not on leads,' according to a note in the programme 'will incur a fine of 50p.) Billy and Nomad pursued her, and several others joined in, taking advantage of the fact that their owners were concentrating on spreading rugs, unpacking hampers, and decanting the port. There followed a period of chaos, outbursts of discipline, and the gradual return of orderly conduct. During the chaos, a weird and horrifying thought occurred to me: what would happen if a lot of lurchers deserted their masters, took to the wilds, and formed a pack? For my part, what would happen is that I would lock myself in the cellar and apply for a military escort. They are all so tough and cunning and hunting-mad. Some of them looked downright vicious. I suspect that in several cases (not ours, of course) it's only the influence of equally tough masters that stops them being fairly nasty. Anyway it may never happen. At this point the judging of the various classes began: I had no time to think about anything else.

It started with the Smooth Dogs, which was where Billy's owner disgraced himself utterly. Charming fellow though he is under normal circumstances, he insisted on being unbelievably earnest about the whole business, which was odd since his own dog, though vastly attractive to other dogs, is no oil painting: a bit heavy at the shoulder, and therefore hard to keep sound; a bit too big and strong to be a proper athlete; and a bad mover. (He's much better since he got stronger, but in those days he moved like a cripple.) However it became immediately apparent that for his master this dog show was serious business. He wore his little tweed cap, and his county-style windcheater, his thornproof trousers, and his brown brogue lace-up boots. A vision of the perfect lurcher-owner. He spent hours washing and combing and brushing the unfortunate Billy; he then proceeded to remind him how he should stand in order to show himself off to the best advantage. Painful minutes as he pulled his nose one way and his tail the other, arranged and rearranged the position of his feet, and tried to make him understand about sticking out his chest and pulling in his stomach. Poor Billy was amazed by the whole performance. ('I really don't know what's got into him. He's not normally like this; he's usually quite a decent bloke. Ouch! Stop that, you bloody moron; it hurts.') The great moment came: the Smooth Dogs were summoned to the judgement. Billy strode into the ring, considerably relieved that the arduous preparation was over. His master paced beside him, as solemn as an undertaker; his gaze never wavered from the straight-ahead position; from time to time, out of the corner of his mouth, he directed clipped imprecations at his hound; I suppose he was saying things like 'Chin up', 'Shoulders square', 'Step lively', and so on. In the middle of the ring the judges eyed the circling contenders and pondered lengthily. The tension grew. Eventually, and very slowly, they began to select those that they wanted to see more of; into the centre crowded the chosen few, the rest stumped disconsolately out of the arena. Among them, alas, was Billy. He took it awfully well; his master, on the other hand, was not so philosophical; as he passed me by, I saw on his face an expression in which incredulity, shock, and bitter hatred had equal shares.

The class was won by the apricot brindle Nomad. Let it be mentioned once (and hereafter never alluded to again) that one of the judges was my Mr Mills, breeder of Rebecca and of Nomad. For a moment I suspected bias, but my suspicions were soon dispelled, for the same set of judges, in the Smooth Bitch class, threw Rebecca into the outer darkness as ruthlessly as they had done Billy.

This was rather a blow but we did not scream about it. Later on we scored a considerable victory. This was in the obedience class. I entrusted Rebecca to the young Miss Gordon for this event, as apparently obedience is not a strong suit with the Gordon whippets (which, now that I come to think about it, is rather surprising). I watched closely from the sidelines, and observed that in this sort of test the only links between dog and handler are psychological or telepathic ones; collars and leads, whips and big sticks are considered *de trop*, and one isn't even allowed to stay close enough to give the beast a discreet kick, should the occasion arise. All that liberty went instantly to Rebecca's head like wine: as soon as she was set free (and despite the fact that all her mates were sitting in a neat little row, gazing in rapt attention at their handlers across the ring), she bolted off the course and fled to my side, very pleased with herself indeed. When it was over, the mistress of ceremonies awarded the first prize to a prince among Jack Russell terriers. (When his master told him to 'stay', he stayed. The judges begged him to move, ordered him to move, and threatened dire punishments if he didn't move; they even tried to bribe him with food. He just yawned in their faces, and waited for the sound of the voice that mattered.) After the second and third prizes, she announced, 'and now a special prize for the most disobedient dog in the class

—Rebecca Simpson!' We advanced amid laughter, accepted congratulations with an attempt at equanimity, and pocketed a one-pound note. It transpired that this was a put-up job organised by Billy's master and mistress to repay me for insults received during the course of the day. Still, a pound's a pound.

What else? Dinah was second in the Veterans, which was robbery, because she was easily the noblest veteran of them all; and Billy, Nomad and Rebecca took part in the racing. For some reason my recollection of the racing is none too clear; I know the dogs were divided into classes by size; Billy and Nomad were in a bigger division than Rebecca. The hare was some sort of hare-like object on the end of a long string. The dogs were lined up, held by their owners. The hare was carried in front of their noses and shaken about in a manner that was intended to send them mad with savage desire; it was then placed in the centre of the track some ten yards ahead of the dogs. A signal was given, the string tightened, the hare shot off, and the dogs were released, What the mechanism was that shifted the hare, I do not know, but it worked admirably; the course was a straight seventy yards or thereabouts. Billy and Nomad both finished out of the money in their race, but Billy beat Nomad, which caused a certain amount of satisfaction in certain quarters. Rebecca treated the whole performance with suspicious aloofness: she lobbed along behind her field, observing, but making no effort to gallop. Her attitude was, as always, "This is something new. I require time to make up my mind about it".

19

I suppose the next major development was the discovery of the 'side-step'. This historic event took place up on the trial-ground one afternoon towards the end of the month. The trial-ground runs along the top of a hill; the valleys that surround it on all sides, and the slopes that lead up to it, are all intensely agricultural, dedicated to the growing of the barley. The backbone of the hill is a mile and a quarter long and roughly a hundred yards wide. Up there, the colour is green, the raw material is downland grass growing where downland grass has always grown, the treatment is cutting and rolling and chain-harrowing and dosing with liberal quantities of peat moss over a period of about a hundred years, the texture is that of a fairly highly-sprung mattress (as you walk, you bounce).

We went there because there is very little protective cover on this smooth green mattress; hares are sensible beasts, and sensible beasts like something to hide behind. Hares would not be up there; they would be placidly chewing away in the depths of the barley. So thought I, and as usual I was wrong. I had overlooked one important factor, the harvest. That very day had brought a rude awakening to the denizens of the fields: hardly had the last drop of dew wilted beneath the rays of the morning sun, when a convoy of combines and tractors and trailers clattered into position and initiated a ruthless 'scorched earth' operation. Or so it must have seemed to those whose larders were being rifled before their very eyes. Apart from the loss of provisions, there was also the very real danger of collision with one of several mechanical monsters, and the animal population must have thought it best to 'up sticks and decamp'. At least one particular hare took refuge on the green sward of the trial-ground, where Rebecca spotted him in no time at all. She froze and stared; the hare stood it for as long as he could, then panicked and fled. Hares do have an odd way of galloping: they never seem to be running at all. One sees them floating through the air with their legs stretched and their ears pointed upwards (or flat along their backs when the pressure is on). Then they hit the ground and simply bounce off again, and so it goes on. Not like a dog: you can see a dog's hind legs stretching forward, his body coiling like a spring. He thrusts forward with his head, neck, and front legs. One can see what makes him run. With a hare, it all seems to be done by hidden springs.

This hare scooted straight up the gallop; Rebecca, well-suited by the good ground, was soon in close attendance. Too close for comfort; the hare turned sharp left, and made for the left-hand boundary of the trial-ground. There he turned right and continued in his original direction. Another hundred yards, and Rebecca closed up; he swerved right and crossed the gallop. Down below, a combine rattled and snorted, so they turned again. They came back down towards me, and passed me, the hare bouncing comfortably, Rebecca all blue eyes and *ventre à terre*. Fifty yards further on, the hare executed a miraculous about-turn; one moment he was galloping one way; the next he was going just as fast in the opposite direction. Rebecca, I noticed, turned well: she lost ground, but she didn't lose her balance; she was turning almost easily, as though she was beginning to know what to expect. They sailed past me and went through the routine all over again: one left turn, three right turns, and back to where I stood. This time I could see that it was serious business: Rebecca was pulling out all the stops and the hare was definitely worried. She was gaining with every stride; then, just when it seemed she had to get him, there was another perfect about-turn, and the hare had a five-yard lead. They galloped up again; the hare was maintaining his advantage, but not increasing it. Then for some reason (maybe he was tiring) he tried the manoeuvre one more time. It was once too often. Rebecca wasn't quite as close to him as before; when he started to turn, she saw what was coming; he turned; she side-stepped; he ran straight into her jaws.

We were well contented when we bore our quarry back into the yard. The yard was decked out in scaffolding, and on the scaffolding were the builders who were gradually restoring the establishment to a reasonable state of repair. As is often the case when builders are working on scaffolding in the sunshine, there was a transistor radio filling the air with music. This particular transistor was situated in the middle of the yard, perched on the wall that surrounded the raised flower-bed. I held up the hare, the men called down their congratulations, Rebecca wandered over to the transistor, cocked her head on one side, and burst into song.

20

At about this time I began to get illusions of grandeur; I became a victim of the idea that I ought to write a book about Rebecca. Previously, I had noted down the things that happened in my diary, simply because I kept a diary of life in general, not particularly for her benefit. As a result of this affliction I scrubbed her out of my diary completely; but whenever she was concerned in anything that I considered noteworthy, I would go to my type-writer and give it the treatment "in depth". Which being the case, I don't see any point in translating the record into 'narrative' at this later date; I can't imagine that my command of the language has noticeably improved in the meanwhile. From time to time I may be forced to insert meaningful asides, but otherwise I have left the record just as it was written at the time. It should positively glow with realism.

29th Sept.
When she has killed a hare after a tough course on a hot afternoon (which is what she did today), she puts her head in the horse-trough, and laps water twenty-one times (twenty-one gulps, that is). After a momentary break, she puts in a thirty-eight lap session. Then a forty-eight, and then a fifty-five. Half an hour later she con-cludes with a final twenty-one. Which goes to show that

coursing is dehydrating.

This particular afternoon, we must have been feeling particularly well; when we crossed the track onto the downs, we both started to run towards the fox-covert. As luck would have it, a hare was sunning himself in our path, and as we were moving a bit we took him by surprise; we were on top of him before he jumped up and ran off. He led us through a series of turns out in the open, followed by a series of turns on the edge of the rough. Not succeeding in shaking off pursuit by these manoeuvres, the hare bolted straight into the middle of the fox-covert, where the grass is waist-high (higher if you're smaller), and the terrain is decorated with abominable thorn bushes, indescribable gorse thickets, treacherous potholes. By this time they were out of sight and I was out of breath, so I decided to continue on my way round the fox-covert, hoping they would rejoin me. I was nearly at the far end, when I caught sight of Rebecca's white nose peering at me over the top of the undergrowth. As she showed no inclination to come to me, I tramped over to her. She was sitting all over her victim, with a very complacent look on her face.

1st October.

Well, now; I know that two things worthy of note have occurred recently, but I am finding it rather difficult to recollect what they were. She caught a mole, but that wasn't one of them. She ran away, but that wasn't one of them either. Now I remember: she bagged a pheasant, a great big juicy cock pheasant, and I made her release it, which she was loath to do, and when eventually I prevailed, she was furious.

We were walking beyond the trial-ground. It was one

of those afternoons that will make people remember 1971's October: bright sunshine, cloudless sky, warm breeze. We were on Mr Harley's land, which was all right while nobody was around, but then a tractor hove into view, going about its business (feeding some cattle, in fact) and I began to feel slightly guilty. I shuffled away from the middle of the stubble and proceeded towards the edge of the field where there was a track. I persuaded her ladyship to stay close, so as to give the impression that we were casually law-abiding. Then a Landrover appeared and crossed our path, and I felt even more out of bounds. Happily no incident took place, and we walked down to the end of the field and joined a cart-track with thick, tussocky downland grass all along the edge.

Rebecca suddenly stopped dead and stared at a particularly large tussock; she stood for about ten seconds quite still, then hurled herself into the air, and landed on it nose first; her nose, in fact, disappeared into it and stayed there. As this is her mole-catching routine, I wasn't unduly impressed. However, as time passed and she made no move of any sort, I decided to investigate. I discovered that the tussock was inhabited by a pheasant, and that Rebecca's teeth were imbedded in some portion of his lower anatomy. As her two front legs were splayed across the rest of him, there was very little he could do. She really didn't want to let go, but finally I managed to prise her jaws apart. The victim exited skywards, screaming his resentment, apparently little the worse for the encounter. Rebecca was spinning round in rage and frustration, and I was doing likewise through fear and embarrassment. Luckily, we were on low ground, out of sight of the tractor and the Landrover, which were over the brow of the hill.

8th October.

Autumn has at last begun; heavy mist in the mornings; chilly until eleven o'clock, after which it becomes tropical. Tropical is how the weather has been these last three weeks. Today she threw herself off the back of Stephen's Landrover, did a somersault, landed on her back and howled (perhaps I should mention the fact that the Landrover was travelling at speed at the time). I was sure she had broken something, but ten seconds later she was bounding about as right as that wet stuff we haven't had much of lately. Stephen has got a four-month-old black Labrador called Maxwell; we walked them up his farm road and back. We gave Rebecca a discipline test and discovered the following: she will 'Sit' if she is right beside me; if she is at a distance, she thinks 'Sit' means 'Come'; so she 'comes' and sits when she gets to me. Remote control doesn't seem to apply.

11th October.

I think she has had a vision, and the doggy God has told her she is destined to be champion hare-catcher of all time; somewhat reminiscent of Joan· of Arc, who was considered mad by many, as is Rebecca. What happened was as follows: we went for our walk today; the clouds were heavy and the drizzle was light. Straightaway I noticed that her ladyship was behaving in an unusual fashion: she kept galloping as fast as she could, hurling herself across the turf in great driving strides, and then throwing herself into skidding turns and flying back the way she had come, for all the world as though there was a hare bobbing along about six inches in front of her nostrils. When she came to the rough, which was tall and wet and most uninviting, she went straight in and hunted

around without a moment's hesitation. Normally, in this sort of weather, she would skulk along at my heels, except if I went through a bad bit, in which case she would daintily circumnavigate it. The final proof of heavenly intervention was when I told her to sit: she was a good thirty yards away from me, and yet she sat, immediately, and without a murmur.

Monday 18th October.
Yesterday she went to London and had a real miserable time of it. When we arrived, hints were dropped to the effect that dogs were not welcome in the house; politely, and in order to give myself time to digest this horrific revelation, I responded with a casual 'she'll be all right in the car.' I was instantly taken at my word, and that was

that. Actually that wasn't entirely that, because my venerable aunt enlarged at length on the reasons why she was anti-dog, *viz.* one, small children are too keen on embracing strange dogs, which could be dangerous (I admit that Rebecca could be described as strange, but only in appearance; her nature—children-wise—is faultless; in fact, she's much better at keeping herself to herself than any child and is far too circumspect to allow any unauthorised embraces); two, strange dogs are too keen on rubbing up against her clothes, and leaving them befurred (no comment). In addition, my cousin Peter didn't help the situation; he would keep mentioning aluminium bowls, in which he suggested I should give her water to drink, after which, he recommended knowingly, I should take her for walks. What with one thing and another, she spent the best part of seven hours tearing the inside of the car to pieces.

She was let out at lunchtime, for a walk and a drink at the pub. We sat outside in the sunshine, and Rebecca immediately showed how useful she is in the matter of picking up birds. We had a long discussion, this bird and I, about her breeding and the extraordinary beauty of her eyes. Many a meaningful glance passed between us, conveying many an unspoken word. The fact that the bird in question was about seventy years of age is neither here nor there. Later on she had another outing, and we walked in Kensington Gardens (my sister, her husband, their baby, Rebecca and I). Rebecca soon had a swarm of doggy admirers; she had a very good gallop and took absolutely no notice of my orders; at one point I thought she was off to Marble Arch with a very saucy Alsatian. Eventually she was forced into a crash-landing (she got too close to me and I tackled her *à la* Rugby); her closest friends were restored to their owners, who turned out to be no less than two beautifully constructed dolly birds. So there! I am the owner of a dog that can pick up dolly birds for me just like that—in Kensington Gardens. The fact that we live in West Wiltshire has nothing to do with it.

Oct 25th.

My friend Jones—(there are four Joneses; father is short and stocky, grey and grizzled. Number one son is tall, dark, and handsome. Number two is tall, fair and moustachioed; he reminds me of an adjutant in a cavalry regiment. Number three is shortish and his fair hair hangs casually round and across a much-lined and weatherbeaten face; unlike the others who are smooth and spruce)—my friend Jones—the tall, dark one—told me the following (when we chanced to meet at the bar of the pub at lunchtime): when dogs were wild and ran in packs, he said, there was a leader who led, and the others who followed. Should one of these step out of line, the leader would discipline him in the following fashion: he would approach the miscreant, apply his teeth to his throat and shake him till his eyes knocked together. Dogs no longer run in packs, he observed, but the instinct lingers on. Therefore, he concluded, when one's dog misbehaves, it is inefficient to beat it. One must grip it by the throat and shake it. Every atom of its being will inform it that it has done wrong and must watch its step in future. This was news to me, and of the most welcome kind; for I loathe beating Rebecca, and she isn't too keen on it herself. I can't wait to get her by the throat.

Found a hare on the plough, but didn't kill it. It seemed to take me hours of puffing and heaving to get myself off the plough, by which time Rebecca was lying exhausted and foiled by the canter round the hill.

(Eight months later: neck-gripping proved ineffective; this is not to say that it is a bad idea; simply that it didn't work on R. But then, what did?)

November 1st.

Yesterday, Sunday, we went hunting. The master of Framfield was the master, his daughters whipped-in, I was the huntsman. Nobody else was invited, because this hunt rarely meets and is very exclusive. The pack consisted of Dinah, Thurber, Icy, Maud, Lucy, two terriers, Mutty and Rebecca; the pack defies description; let me say only that it was wide-ranging in sizes and shapes. Incidentally, Maud is Dinah's grand-daughter and lovely. The meet was at Kimpton Down at 3.30 p.m. A warm, cloudy day; slight breeze; good scent.

Put the hounds into the stubble, beyond the Clump,

above the gallops. Hounds worked well; hunt-servants impeccably behaved. After a hundred yards, up gets a hare; one hallooooh, whole pack on as one; two turns, one bleat, and she's a goner.

Another fifty yards, another hare gets up; several hollers, increasing in intensity and indignation; no hounds on; hare canters away laughing audibly.

Lost hound (Mutty) puts an end to proceedings, and all concerned return to base gladly rejoicing. Mutty is already *in situ* when we get there, so all is well. Rebecca is awarded the mask, pads, brush and all that goes between, for good behaviour and keenness (or because somebody preferred that somebody else should have the pleasure of gutting, skinning, etc.).

Tuesday, 9th Nov.

Her birthday is Sunday next. I drove my friend Stephen to lunch at the pub. He lost his driving licence as a result of a series of misdemeanours, and goes lunchtime-hungry when he cannot find a lunchtime-chauffeur. Today he was in luck, and I returned him, bulging slightly more than usual, to his office at the farm. As I was driving away, I had a thought, and stopped and hooted. He came to the door.

'I think I'll walk Rebecca up the farm, if that's all right.'

'Certainly. Why not take Maxwell?'

'Is there anywhere you don't want walked on?'

'No. Go where you like.'

Maxwell, the black Labrador, is now about four months old. Very soft and plump. Rebecca seems to bully him a lot, but he doesn't mind. Anyway, when it comes to thick, thorny hedgerows, he shows her up no end. He goes straight into the thickest, most off-putting bits, and she stands and looks, puts her nose in and then backs out, looks at me, and eventually follows him, but can't get out quick enough. Also, he's rather clever: he realises that she is very keen on games, and that it takes two to play; so he makes her do all the work. She rushes off, looking at him over her shoulder, challenging him to chase her; whereupon he lies down. She turns and comes galloping back, and when she gets within range, he launches himself into the air, hits her amidships and knocks her over. She gets up, shakes herself and runs off; he lies down again, and the performance repeats itself.

We did the hedgerow along the lane, and then we did a field full of cows; both dogs behaved with commendable control and detachment. Then we started to hunt across a field that had just been cultivated, and immediately a hare got up and fled. They turned it together once; then Rebecca closed up on it; it turned and found it was heading straight for Maxwell, which made it change direction fast, and it dived through the fence with both dogs hot on its heels. When I got to the fence, I found it was three strands of barbed wire, plus a layer of sheepwire, so they had done well. I climbed over, pushed through the thorns. There they were, halfway across the next field, in possession of their quarry. There was a tractor cultivating, and if he had happened to be looking in the right direction, the driver must have seen a lovely hunt.

I told them how good they were, and that they couldn't eat it there and then, which they were reluctant to believe, and then we set off home. On the way a hare got up, but they didn't see it, and I didn't say anything because I reckoned they had done enough for one day. Anyway we sauntered across to where the hare had been; when we got there, Rebecca immediately put her nose down and took off. She followed the scent through the wire, along a fence, through it, and across another field before she finally lost it. She really has many talents.

When we got back to base, I washed the plough off her legs and feet. She spent the rest of the afternoon stretched out in front of the electric fire, a picture of virtuous contentment.

(Note 1. This was the first time she hunted with another dog. Even though Maxwell was hardly the ideal team-mate, his presence made all the difference; the effort was cut by half. I renewed my resolve that in future I must try to find dogs for her to work with. However, persuading her to work with other dogs was another matter. I found that when she was in company, she was very reluctant to do anything but play games with her 'friend'.

Note 2. Maxwell is a highly bred gun-dog. Only time will tell whether this early training as a lurcher has absolutely ruined him as a gun-dog. I do hope not.)

21

On Tuesday, Nov. 16th Rebecca became a shooting dog for the first time; not without some trepidation on the part of her connections. I, for example, had heard so much about something called 'running on', and had seen the extreme severity with which Rebecca's friend Athos had been treated when he 'ran on' and also for that matter when he 'ran off'! A dog can't win, it seems to me, where shooting is concerned. (Athos, by the way, is the spaniel who replaced Titus the whippet.)

We—the beaters, that is, and assorted dogs—entered a wood at Manton, and began to make our noisy way towards the guns, who were posted, in treacherous concealment, along the far end. At first I kept Rebecca on her lead; but we kept tying ourselves in knots, and together, and to trees), and our progress, though good-humoured, was laborious and slow. Eventually I got to thinking about it, and reasoned as follows: The guns are at the far end, ready, and waiting. Therefore what does it matter how fast or how far Rebecca progresses? To think is definitely not to act, so I just tentatively sounded out the views of my fellow beaters (all of whom had years of experience of situations like this). They concurred with my reasoning, so I took fate in my hands and loosed her off. Shame on me for my lack of faith! She was perfectly all right. She galloped about the undergrowth, making a very satisfactory racket; she played with the other dogs (but not enough to distract them); and when I called she came to me, which meant that she never got too far ahead of the line. My other trepidation was lest the noise of gunfire should dement her. No trouble at all; she couldn't have cared less.

She had two moments of glory, both later in the day, when we were up at lovely Slinford. The first happened thus: we had beaten along a hedgerow with no very noticeable success, and were congregated in a cluster of guns, beaters, and dogs, before going off to the next batt-lefield. We were standing just above a disused sunken track, all overgrown and wild, which had been beaten through, and shot over, as the finale of the previous oper-ation. Suddenly Rebecca crouched and peered and then leapt. It was her well-known mole-catcher. However this was no ordinary mole. As she landed, nose first, there was an indignant scream, a fanfare of plumage, and a discomfited hen-pheasant rocketed into the air. The gun-nery, alas, did not live up to the doggery, and the bird escaped.

Later, we were beating along a high bank above the farm road. On the road was Paul, 'armed escort' to the beaters (and also squire of Manton, Seigneur of Slinford, and proud owner of Athos, the champion running-on spaniel); ostensibly his job was to assault any birds that tried to fly back, instead of flying forward to where the heavy artillery was deployed; in fact, I think he was there to rescue any beater who looked like being molested by our feathered enemies (the birds up on these Wiltshire mountains are of fantastic size and strength, and inordi-nately bad-tempered, especially when they suspect that someone is out to 'do' them). The only other possible explanation of his presence (nor is it an unreasonable one) is that he thought the beaters, if left to their own devices, might slack, shirk, or strike. He has a healthy interest in getting his money's worth; he once complained bitterly that he was being cheated, because he noticed that one of his men had the strength to walk home at the end of a day's work. Whatever the true reason, there he was, and at a given moment he said to me, 'I believe she's found one.' I followed his gaze; Rebecca was crouching before a bush, or tuft, or shrub; she was staring at it intently, not to say unwaveringly. There followed the by now well-known curve through the air, and lo!, a cock-bird fought its way out of her grasp and into the great blue yonder. It cleared the trees, reached the heights, paddled up over the valley, levelled off into a fierce gliding dive, or rather diving glide (actually it was a fast glide in a slightly downward direction), and made for the cover of a wood. It was above the nearest trees when the shot came: it shuddered, stopped, changed before our eyes from a flying machine into a clumsy, shapeless mass, which fell into the branches, and thence to the ground.

Rebecca was very brave all day, and went through some pretty nasty places. When we got home, she had a cut on her chest; nothing to worry about, purely superficial, more of a graze really, but indubitably a sign of extraordinary virtue.

22

Nov. 30th. St Andrew's day.

'Let's see if we can't get one more Darlingsford hare' was the rather sad theme for today. Sad to be leaving, and sad to be putting Rebecca in Kennels until I find if I can decently keep her at Framfield. I was leaving because of circumstances, my circumstances, which I had allowed to get out of hand and to become, consequently, not quite what I wanted. It was like this: apart from the hours I spent out in the open (generally with Rebecca) and working with the horses, I also spent a considerable proportion of each day in an office wrestling with various problems like somebody's tax rebate and code number, somebody else's leaking roof, a third person's medical certificate, and a never-ending stream of cess-pits that were always overflowing. The outdoor side of life made up for a lot of this sort of thing, but the time came when I found I was taking the problems of the office out onto the downs with me, and that they were interfering with my pleasures. The fault was mine, because one should always be able to separate work from play and not let either affect the other; however, there it was, and I decided that changes must be made. I arranged to 'retire' to Framfield, where I could justify my existence by riding out, helping with the horses, and generally making myself useful; at the same time I would have a complete rest from cess-pits, medical certificates, leaking roofs, code numbers and tax rebates; this holiday to continue until I felt like diving back into the hurly-burly of real life. (Note: the prescription was not entirely unsuccessful; after a few weeks of placid rustic pursuits, I felt the old zest stir, stretch, and shake itself; a few more weeks and I found myself with not enough to do. It was then that I turned out my old diary and my typewritten sheets and started to put this volume together.)

My apprehension about a home for Rebecca is due to the fact that I am not sure where exactly I shall be living at Framfield or for how long. (Note: seven months later and I am still there.) In addition there is the beloved Hettie, who wanders at will where she pleases and is respected by all who know her; Rebecca, alas, has shown signs of 'not knowing' her, except when she is aware that she is being watched; I cannot be confident about watching her adequately while I am working. The master and mistress of Framfield are going away for a week's holiday, and the thought of greeting them on their return with the news that Rebecca has casually murdered Hettie is a prospect that I find too painful to contemplate. So she goes to Mrs Herron on Friday until I work something out.

We drove down the Galton road to the lay-by, where we left the car and headed North. Darlingsford stretches East to West, and all the natural walks are along those lines; this means that on a Winter's afternoon the sun is dead in one's eyes as one goes out and one can't see a thing. That's why I drove West, and hunted from South to North. We went across the middle and 'did' the valley. Blue sky with wisps of cloud, a fresh breeze, visibility good. Nothing stirred except a dozen partridges, so we made a big circle and started back.

We got as far as the top of the bank; the bank where all the horses do their final scamper the day before they run. Three furlongs of springy turf stretching down to our left; it ended on our right where the rough begins and extends up to the top of Slinford. The hare got up about two hundred yards from the end of the gallop; Rebecca was straight on to him. She turned him at the top and they headed down towards me; he turned again, and they crossed in front of me. They headed back towards the rough, but turned before reaching it. Down again, left into the rough, right out of it, and back to where I stood. Turn again, back up again, and the hare disappeared into the long grass. I saw Rebecca leaping up to see over the top of the undergrowth and galloping off almost before she hit the ground again. I stopped running because I knew she would lose him, and also because my chest was wheezing like an ancient steam-engine. I walked up to the corner and waited. Normally she has a wild gallop round to work off her disappointment and then comes back to me. I looked down into the valley but didn't see her. After a few minutes I thought to myself 'maybe she's gone off towards the top,' as that's the way the hare would probably have gone. I had a good look, but couldn't see anything because of the sun. I climbed over the wire, and started ambling up the hill, squinting horribly. Then I saw her; a hazy black silhouette cantering down towards me. She dipped down off the horizon, and I could see her better: she wasn't cantering, she was going flat out, and the hare was no more than three yards ahead of her. The ground was full of holes and hollows and ridges; the hare was twisting and turning in desperation, but losing ground all the time. After four or five skidding, sliding turns, she had him.

Extraordinary hound: she had two lie-downs, and two

good blows, and then she was off again. Usually, it's taken her about a quarter of an hour to get her breath back, and she's never had such a long course as this; I suppose she's getting stronger all the time.

As we trudged back across the downs to the lay-by, I saw the gallop-man working on the hill. We went over and I showed him the hare. 'How about that?' said I.

He gazed at me with eyes filled with wonder. He said, 'Before I forget, my cess-pit's overflowing. Could you please have it emptied.' At that moment I knew, with an absolute certainty, that it was time to get out.

Later the same day: when she is tired but for some reason doesn't want to go to sleep, like after a long course late in the afternoon, when her stomach is telling her that dinner will soon be ready and she doesn't want to miss it, she is quite funny to watch: she lies on the sofa and her eyes begin to close. Then she shakes herself, and raises her head erect, and stares into the distance. Then her eyes shut again, and her head begins to nod. It sinks till it's almost resting on her knees, and then she heaves it up again and opens her eyes with an effort. So it goes on, until finally she gives in: she crosses her front legs, rests her chin on her paws, sticks her nose down the back of the sofa, swallows noisily, utters one long grunt of resignation and falls asleep.

23

On the 4th of December I left Darlingsford and moved to Framfield. Rebecca spent a week in kennels ('such an intelligent dog; never stops stealing things') and joined me on about the 11th. From then until January 19th was a period of unparalleled misery for me, and of unending drama for her. Naturally it was all her fault, and just as naturally nothing that happened worried her one little bit.

I ceased typing out descriptions of Rebecca's memorabilia as they occurred partly because there were too many of them, mainly because they were so horrifying that I couldn't bring myself to write them down at length. Just a few furtive jottings were all I managed. Now that the storm has passed, those furtive jottings (which bring back such vivid recollections that, even now I shudder) form the basis of the concluding chapters.

On the first Saturday morning after her arrival, the master of Framfield took her with all the other dogs to have a run on the gallops while the horses did their work. The dogs always stay with him while he organises the work, and then follow the Landrover when he drives down to the far end to watch the horses as they finish. This arrangement was not good enough for Rebecca; she saw me on a horse and she came to my side, and stayed with me despite all suggestions, entreaties, and threats.

This meant that when I, along with about fifteen others, cantered one and a quarter miles, she cantered one and a quarter miles. As long as she stayed with me it wasn't too bad: I cantered along hurling abuse at her, and she gazed up at me with her big blue eyes and didn't take a blind bit of notice! The trouble began when she found that I wasn't going fast enough; then she left me, proceeded up to the head of the string, and started to snap at the heels of the leading horse. Unfortunately he didn't kick her, so she jumped up and grabbed his tail. This was much more fun, so she did it again; then she very considerately slowed down so that she could tell me all about it. It was thus that we strode past the trainer.

After that she was banned from the gallops, which was not the end of our troubles but more like the beginning. I used to leave her in the office or in the lads' mess with instructions that she was to be released after the horses had left the yard. I didn't like to suggest a longer stay,

because she was still just a little bit of an unknown quantity, house-training-wise, and also because she was quite likely to start singing if she became frustrated. So she would stay indoors for about a quarter of an hour, and then be released, and she would find the place bereft of horses, people and dogs. Then she would become *très ennuyée*. But not for long: she soon found ways and means of filling the vacuum.

24

The blow fell one grey December morning, when the mistress of Framfield beckoned me into an empty segment of the office and said enigmatically:

'There's a deputation coming.'

'A deputation?'

'From the village.'

'A deputation from the village?'

'Mrs Grey told me this morning.'

Mrs Grey is charming and cooks the best mince pie I ever hope to eat, and would not spread terrifying propaganda without good reason.

'It's about the chickens,' added the chatelaine.

I began, rather unwillingly, to understand.

'Rebecca?' I casually hazarded a guess.

'Well, they do say it's the blue-eyed one,' admitted the bearer of the tidings. Such beautiful blue eyes, such unusual blue eyes; so many people had insisted that no other dog existed with eyes of that particular shade of blue. What a give-away, what a terrible mistake they were.

'Shall I go and see them?' said I, gazing down the drive and wondering how many minutes were left to us before the angry throng began to swarm up it. Would there be time enough to buy them off, and soften their vengeful, murderous rage with a smile here, a friendly word there, and a handful of pound notes *partout*? 'Do nothing,' advised my counsellor. 'Do nothing, but gang warily,' or words to that effect; so warily we ganged, Rebecca and I, and no siege developed, and the subject of deputations practically disappeared from local conversation.

But not for long. Maybe we relaxed our precautions; maybe Rebecca became more adept at escaping from her various prisons; maybe there was in fact another blue-eyed dog in the area. Whatever the truth of the matter, ten days later my unfortunate hostess was telling me (and with some justifiable irritation) of a second threatened deputation. This time, in addition to the litany of crimes committed, and the *bona fides* of the identification, there was a new factor—evidence, *viz. corpus delicti*: the corpse of a white chicken lay in the middle of the village street, and had been seen by lads riding by on their way back to the yard. My blood ran cold, as did, no doubt, that of the chicken. Rebecca yawned. My counsellor once again dissuaded me from throwing myself on the mercy of the peasants. This time, she suggested, it would be too dangerous in view of the aggravated situation, and I think she was right.

I said that word should be sent to the enemy that the dog in question was not a native Framfield dog, but a visiting Simpson, and this suggestion was carried out, with the rider (or postscript) that deputations should therefore not proceed up the front drive to Framfield House, but up the back lane to The Croft, where I lived. Nothing disenthuses a potential deputy like the prospect of a back lane; or so it seemed, for no deputation appeared.

Curious to relate, about this time Rebecca started wearing her collar again; on it is a plaque naming her and giving her Darlingsford address. This must have pretty effectively confused the opposition, certainly it substantiated the claim that she was not a Framfield dog; which I think must have been the intention, as it certainly wasn't me that buckled it round her neck. Mind you, I did what I could; I even adopted the practice of shutting her up, during the day, in the fully furnished coal shed in which she had her sleeping quarters. Unfortunately it had a broken window, and each time I put her in, she slipped out again.

The third time that my mentor summoned me to conference (about a week later), deputations were a thing of the past. This time, she had it on Mrs Grey's unimpeachable authority, it was the police. The village was going to report Rebecca to the police, and if we didn't look out, repent, and mend her manners, she would be convicted of chicken-killing, and, being beyond parental control, would be condemned to death.

Before it's too late, I said to myself, something must be done. I blocked the gap in the window of her prison; Rebecca promptly ate her way through the barrier. But I caught her before any further disaster could be attributed to her, and employed the local carpenter-cum-handyman to do a professional job of it. Rebecca ripped his work apart in about five minutes. Once again she was recaptured with her reputation intact (up to a point). Then I got the biggest, thickest, toughest length of teak-like timber, and four of the fiercest nails in the district; at last I was successful. The air was filled with the muffled screams of her frustration—I laughed. I laughed because I had beaten her, and also because, after weeks of worry and trepidation, I was now able to ride out and do my work without having to wonder what devilry she might be up to.

25

That was the main story of those particular weeks, but there were other minor sagas. The yearlings used to go out third lot, about twelve o'clock; they exercised in the paddock behind the yard. Rebecca soon became aware of this fact, and when they appeared, she appeared. She would spring out and chase them, and they would scoot off in all directions, much to the surprise and discomfort of their jockeys, who would scream and swear at her, and then scream and swear at me when we met for lunch. Yearlings scoot quite enough without any help from a dog, so I was more than sympathetic; however, this didn't seem to improve the situation. Her finest moment (or rather, the one she will remember with the most pride) was when she grabbed a cantering yearling filly by the tail, and remained attached for a reputed fifteen strides; as always, she survived unscathed.

I devoted long hours of deep thought to this problem. At length I came up with what I hoped would be the answer. In an adjoining paddock there were three ponies turned out: a tiny bay, a small grey, and a considerably larger grey. This last was quite big enough for me to ride; he belonged to a child from a nearby village, who was allowed to keep him in that particular paddock. I calculated that if I could get the freedom of the pony, and the freedom of the Long Tom (or hunting whip), I could ride the one, and beat my dog with the other, as and when she was stupid enough to have a go at me (or rather, at my steed). Messages were passed back and forth, and the pony was made available; representations to the trainer and the head lad secured the Long Tom; considerable time was devoted to improving my aim (I had been warned, and I found it to be true, that if one is inexperienced in such matters, one can do considerable damage with a Long Tom; but only to oneself or to one's horse). In time, the preparations were completed; and at no stage was Rebecca allowed to get an inkling of what was going on. The great day arrived; in one hand I carried a bucket of oats; under the other arm I clutched the saddle, the bridle, and the instrument of torture; at my heels trotted the unsuspecting hound. We arrived at the centre of the paddock; I laid my tack on the ground and rattled the bucket of oats; the ponies looked up, took notice, and hurried across; Rebecca watched the proceedings with intelligent interest. When the ponies arrived, I captured the one I was after, and diverted the others with the oats which I poured in two heaps on the ground. They began to eat; I began to saddle up their friend, who was fairly choked at not being permitted to join the others. At this point Rebecca, who doesn't like oats anyway, decided it was time for a game; she darted round in front of the smallest pony, and flattened herself in the grass, in her 'come and get me' position. The pony continued to munch steadily. She sprinted behind him, and gave him another chance; he remained unimpressed. One more half-circle to the front: still no reaction; back behind she went; I was thinking 'You won't be playing these games much longer' or something along those lines, when the pony intervened; he gazed at her under his belly, between his legs (without ever missing a munch), then, as she leapt up to continue the game, he let fly with one thunderbolt blow from his off-hind. It caught her in the ribs, sent her flying through two graceful somersaults, and landed her wailing mightily some ten yards away. She screamed like a stuck pig; I felt rather foolish: after all my planning, and organising, and practising, the whole job had been done to a nicety by one little bay pony, in no time at all, and without the least bit of fuss or bother. Feeling rather superfluous, I completed my tacking-up, got on the pony, and cantered round Rebecca, inviting her to come and play; she wouldn't come near me; in fact she hobbled away whimpering pitifully.

'She's cured,' said I, often, and to all and sundry. 'Completely cured. She'll never chase a horse again.' So, naturally, the next morning she was allowed to join the other dogs on the gallops. When the horses cantered, I watched her with feelings of deep satisfaction, and I couldn't believe my eyes; the moment she saw them, she was off like an arrow in pursuit and chased them every yard of the way; she was about as cured as a measles epidemic. All that she had learned was to keep a healthy distance from their hooves. I suppose it shows her intelligence, but it was scant consolation for me at the time. I had a lot of explaining to do, my apologies were not very well received, and Rebecca was banished once again to the coal shed.

This merely meant that her chances of unescorted adventures were minimal; and when they occurred she made the most of them. Like the time the gallop-man came to me in the yard, and announced between hoots of laughter that he had something to report. It transpired that he had been standing in his garden minding his own business when Rebecca appeared. She made her way into the garden opposite, and proceeded, with the fluency that comes from long experience, to devour a selection of assorted goodies that had been put out for the birds. At this point the owner of the property appeared and discovered her. I understood that she was a large lady of definite views and considerable dignity, and that she was not amused. 'Hopping mad she was,' reported the gallop-man. 'Hopping mad. Silly old cow'.

There may well have been reverberations, but they weren't strong enough to upset my apple-cart. We had ironed out the major points of contention, and we ironed out a few more, and then we settled down to an era of almost unbelievable tranquillity. Rebecca promenaded in the early morning gloom while I mucked out. (Actually, it wasn't quite as simple as that: we would emerge together from our house, Rebecca all bright-eyed and bushy-tailed, me slightly less eager and a great deal more sleepy; then she would disappear round the corner, and I would spring suddenly and rather painfully to life; the morning air would ring to a stream of abuse as I hurled myself in pursuit; the winning post was the dog-kennel; if she got there first, she would devour Hettie's new-laid egg; if I did, it was saved, and the master of Framfield had it for his breakfast, and Rebecca was in a furious temper all morning. Having completed this little ritual, she did her promenading, and I did my mucking out.) She was then locked up for the rest of the morning. Towards midday she would register her displeasure by howling, but that cut no ice with me (or with any of her friends). During the rest of the day she would accompany me, and we went for regular walks to keep her in good condition. Unfortunately, the Framfield gallops were very short of hares, and we didn't have much sport. In the evening, all the dogs were fed together, and she would usually sneak into the house with the others, and stretch herself on a sofa to rest in comfort. I can't say I was particularly keen to stop this practice, because it left me free to sally forth to the pub, or to the cinema, or to the dining room of various friends. About ten o'clock I would go round and collect her, walk her, and shut her up for the night.

26

One afternoon Rebecca and I and an American youth called Mike, who had the doubtful pleasure of living with us for a couple of months, were watching racing on T.V. I, as is my custom on dull afternoons when the racing is ordinary, was dozing. I remember being vaguely aware that Mike had let Rebecca out; I wondered what she would find to amuse herself with; I remember feeling too sleepy to do anything about it, and then I dozed off again.

A knock on the door roused me. 'Your dog's killed one of Jerry's chickens,' was the message. Jerry and his wife catered for the living-in lads; they kept chickens and pigs round the back. Up till now, Rebecca had studiously avoided his property. However, they were on holiday that week, and Rebecca was never slow to seize an opportunity. Jerry had peculiarly dark eyes: they shine when he is in a good mood, they glow dully when he is drunk, and they glitter wickedly when he is angry. As things stood, it seemed odds on him being very angry when he returned, which was a prospect that filled me with depression. 'Here we go again,' I thought to myself.

It transpired that the blacksmith's apprentice had been a witness to the deed, as had the head lad. I started with the apprentice, and found him, oddly enough, in the forge. 'She had it,' he confirmed, 'and half killed it.' I asked him where the unfortunate corpse was. 'It was still alive, so I threw it back into the run. It flopped down and the others started pecking at it,' he said. It crossed my mind that he might well have wrung its neck, and put it out of its misery. It also crossed my mind that I had better go and do just that myself. Apart from humanitarian considerations, I had an ulterior motive for wishing it dead; I had been told that a dead chicken, immovably attached to the neck of its murderer and left there till it rots, cures dogs of that particular vice like no other remedy. (Talking of remedies, my friend Ian told me that he once had a young shooting dog; this shooting dog didn't kill sheep, didn't worry sheep, and didn't chase sheep; it just looked at sheep in an odd sort of way, which he, being educated in these matters, recognised as boding no good. 'It's a terrible thing,' said he. 'A terrible thing if a dog starts being interested in sheep. It must be stopped before it starts.' 'What did you do?' I asked. It seemed that on the farm where he lived there was a barn; it had loose-boxes along both sides and a narrow passage down the middle, linking two yards. He tied the dog up in the middle of the passage and proceeded to drive two hundred sheep over it from one yard to the other, and back again, and several times more. It didn't surprise me to learn that the dog was a confirmed sheepophobiac from then on. Incidentally, I reflected that dog-training is much easier if one can lay one's hands, without too much effort, on a couple of yards, a barn, and two hundred or so sheep.)

Where was I? On my way to apply the ultimate quietus to a very unhappy chicken I met the head lad, who repeated the 'half dead' diagnosis, but when I got to the scene of the crime dusk had fallen, and no corpse was visible.

Next day I learned that, in Jerry's absence, one Kelsey was in charge of the livestock, so I commissioned him to retrieve the remains and bring them to me. I then went out for the afternoon. When I returned, the American told me the following. Kelsey had appeared soon after lunch; Mike opened the door to him.

'I've brought a chicken for Andrew.'

Mike looked at it and said, 'He wants a dead chicken. That's a live one.'

'That's the one his dog had. It's lost all its tail feathers, and it's a bit scratched.'

'Well, he can't tie that round her neck, that's for sure.'

'Shall I kill it?'

'No.'

I was disappointed at not being able to carry out my experiment, but overjoyed that the bird had survived. The angry glitter in those peculiarly dark eyes is something I can well do without. Kelsey disinfected the bird's laceration with something from the horses' veterinary cupboard, and it was well on its way towards recovery before its owner returned.

(Note: The truth of the matter, as I was slowly beginning to realise, is as follows: a high-bred lurcher is a dog that is bred to lurch; that means, to steal everything that is stealable, and to chase everything that moves; both these talents are instinctive. For example, I sometimes go onto the gallops on foot, and I keep Rebecca on a lead. When the horses start to work, I tell her to sit and she sits. When they come past us, she squirms, moans, pulls against the lead, looks up at me, sits down again, and keeps on like that until they disappear; although I realise that my understanding of dogs is minimal, I am quite convinced that she simply cannot help this terrific urge to pursue. Which being the case, if these instincts are not controlled and harnessed and directed along reasonable lines, the fault is the owner's—which is rather a frightening thought.)

143

27

On Thursday 20th January I was deeply in love, which, as far as I am concerned, is not just a dirty word, but an enviable experience which has an exquisitely entrancing side to it; there are, it is true, other sides to it, which one must never forget, not even when one has been irretrievably bowled over, and is completely off balance. But, as I say, there is an entrancing side to it, and that's the side that I was on, on this particular Thursday. It was my good fortune to be lunching with the object of my passion and also with two evil-looking men, which is not the ideal arrangement, but one cannot always have everything one's own way. Actually they were not in the least bit evil-looking (one of them was Maxwell's owner, whom I have gone to considerable lengths on several occasions in earlier chapters to describe in the most flattering term), but under such circumstances one is inclined to look askance, and darkly, at anyone who is within hand-clasping distance of the loved one. We billed, cooed, gazed meaningfully and sighed audibly; we also put paid to a vast quantity of beef and onion pie. Afterwards, it transpired that the men were obliged to go about their business, and that we, the beloved and I, had an hour or so to kill. She was small, fair, and beautifully made, and the afternoon was misty but not too dark, so we decided to walk the dogs, namely Rebecca, her friend Maxwell, and a one-eyed collie. Many people may think it unlikely that one could be in raptures about the owner of a collie with one eye, on the grounds that a single eye is rather creepy, and that the creeps are not conducive to romance. I tell you now, it doesn't make the slightest difference, not if it's the real thing.

'Follow me,' said I, for she had her own car. I led her to the Darlingsford roundabout (we had lunched just down the road), headed towards Galton, and stopped at the lay-by halfway along the downs.

We set off through the mist and stopped when we saw a grey shape that turned into a tractor and trailer and the gallop-man, whom I hadn't seen since he mentioned his cess-pit and I promptly left Darlingsford. This time we talked of other things, and I asked his leave to be on the downs (for I was now a long-gone has-been). Then we carried on until the beloved complained of cold feet, which suggested that, however smitten I was by her, she was not exactly walking on air over me. We stopped and turned and started to retrace our steps; the dogs were milling about in the mist, but when one is in love one doesn't pay too much attention to dogs. Thus it wasn't until we were quite close to the road that we noticed that Rebecca was missing. I hollered and whistled, but she didn't respond; I made disparaging comments about her contrary nature, but that didn't do any good either. I began to run out of conversation; the silence became ominous; I was conscious that cold feet must surely be getting colder; some sort of distraction was urgently required. Weakly and with the minimum of conviction I said something like 'wouldn't it be thrilling if she was hunting something, and brought it right over here and killed it at our feet?' At the time, I thought a heavy cold was the most thrilling thing that was likely to happen to us, and I deeply regretted the unnecessary reference to feet. However, suddenly the mist lifted slightly and we saw her galloping through some trees on top of a small tumulus about seventy yards away. 'Was that something running in front of her?' I asked, but we couldn't be sure. She galloped down off the tumulus, and started a left-handed turn towards us across some wild, tall downland. Then a fine hare broke out onto the gallops and Rebecca was close behind him. They crossed in front of us, turned left back onto the tumulus and disappeared over the other side. I ran across, climbed up among the trees, and when I reached the top I saw her lying in the grass about fifty yards away. Maxwell was with her, and I could hear the horrid squeaking of a captive hare. I cantered over and broke its neck.

How can I convey the emotions of that moment, without being accused of exaggeration verging on the hysterical? Let me put it this way: ever since we moved to Framfield, that dog had made me sweat horribly; her daytime outrages successfully ruined my days, and formed the basis of the nightmares that ruined my nights; all in all, the time was rapidly approaching when I would have to face the fact that I hated the sight of her (up to a point). Yet all it took was one short (mainly invisible) course, and all the unforgivable and unforgettable crimes were, in a flash, forgiven and forgotten. Rebecca was reinstated; her pedestal was, if anything, loftier than before. As for the loved one, 'deeply impressed' is, I think, not too strong an expression to use.

On the evening of Wednesday, 26th January (the night after Alan Rudkin retained his title at the Albert Hall, and I was there) Rebecca entertained her friends to jugged hare. The hare was jugged by Mrs Bye, whose culinary talents are venerated by those who know her;

she came out of retirement especially for the occasion, and said it was a fine hare, which was good enough for me. She cooked it in a large colander in her cottage; I collected it, and reheated it at Framfield while I, with my own hands, cooked the vegetables; these were leaf spinach, and potatoes lightly boiled, halved, and fried in oil till they are crisp and golden (which is how I like potatoes). The wine was red and plentiful and slipped down with no trouble at all; but I don't recall its name. Five people attended the feast: the master of Framfield, who had put up with so many of Rebecca's misdemeanours with such saintly equanimity (his wife chose to dine on a pork chop; she doesn't like hare); the doctor who had prescribed for her droopy ear so many months before; the doctor's wife, my friend Ian, and me. A fair cross-section of civilised society; all were unanimous in their praise of the grub. The colander held enough for five, with seconds for those who wanted. What was left fed Rebecca twice.

Rebecca behaved in her usual unpredictable fashion. At one point early in the evening, she strolled out of the drawing room, paused in the hall to stare into the kitchen, where the action was, and then wandered towards the front door. Some minutes later, one of the humans did much the same thing, and chanced upon evidence of an indiscretion committed on the mat by a dog. All the other dogs had alibis. It was one of the tidier messes, and easily disposed of; a careful gathering up of the mat, followed by a wristy flick, and it flew, leaving no trace, into the outer darkness. Rebecca was not proceeded against; after all, she had tried to catch one's eye, but one was too busy with the potatoes and the leaf spinach; and she had gone very properly to the door, only nobody was there to open it; how could one blame her? In addition, I got the feeling that this was no ordinary mess; that it was significant, as though the beast was trying to tell us something, and did it in the only way she knew how. *Memento mori* is what I rather think the Romans would have called it, a reminder of mortality, fallibility, and imperfection, at a time when things are looking particularly immortal, infallible, and perfect. Rebecca was, I think trying to warn her friends against allowing jugged hare to go to their heads. Things may look good tonight, she implied, but don't forget that we've had our bad times before, and we'll surely have them again. What better way to drive the lesson home than by a portentous mess on the mat.

For the rest of the evening she stretched herself out in front of the fire, and behaved very like Queen Victoria in one of her better moods: she took an interest in all that was happening, was courteous to her guests, and modestly acknowledged the compliments that were showered upon her.

(Note: six months later: where was the beloved, and why no explanation of her absence, nor, indeed, any mention of her at all? I suspect that at the time the subject rankled, irritated, and annoyed, and was therefore excluded from the story. Now the passage of time has allowed the wound to heal. If it must be told, it must be told: she preferred to spend the evening in the steaming arms of a Lambourn jockey [I mentioned that she was small], swaying to the rhythm of a Swindon discotheque. These things happen.)

28

Here I sit, wilting beneath the ruthless pounding of a hangover, pathetically attempting to get this finished in time. Time has seven days to go, and I have only one more chapter to write, so it shouldn't be impossible, although typewriting with a hangover feels (I imagine) rather like shooting oneself in the head with a machine-gun and forgetting to stop. Today's hangover is the result of last night's outing to a jazz club, which featured the Johnnie Bastable Five (or six, or seven), George Melly, and several large whiskies. George Melly has been singing jazz for ages (I heard a whisper that it was he who put the Mel- into Melpomene, but that may be stretching it a bit); at any rate, I used to listen to him with great pleasure, in my long-lost youth. When I read in the local paper that he was appearing down here, I said to myself 'Jazz singers improve (so I am led to believe) with age and experience and the influence of life's rich pageant; he was good in the old days; maybe now he will be even better.' Nor was I disappointed; Mr Melly warbled like the proverbial gravel-mouthed nightingale; Mr Bastable and his friends did their thing in exemplary fashion; the whisky slipped down with unusual facility. I don't regret a moment of it, not even this morning as I wilt.

Where was I? I was in the middle of a ploughed field,

on the afternoon of a rainy day in March. Spring threatened to be just round the corner; its coming inspired in me no feelings of pleasant anticipation; I saw it, not as the beginning of summer, but as the end (for the time being) of coursing, which I wasn't ready for. I hadn't yet managed to achieve one of the major projects of the Winter, which was to find a friend for Rebecca to hunt with, to persuade her to hunt with this friend without messing about all the time, to find a hare with both dogs equally involved, and to let her discover and appreciate the value of a partner. Time was running short and I began to fear that her future education would have to wait till the Autumn. But then Billy intervened, and it became apparent that there was still a chance. It transpired that his owner had the same feelings about the Spring as I did; he too wanted to have one more go before we called it a day; as a result, there we were, in the rain, on the plough, one Sunday afternoon in March. (Incidentally, some people say that there is no close season for coursing; they opine that one should refrain during the hare's courting, mating, and breeding season; otherwise, they course all the year round. Myself, I can't see it: I don't think it's much fun coursing when the corn is high, because you keep losing hares in it; and no fun at all in hot weather, when the dog nearly explodes if asked to gallop any distance at all.

It was a long field on the side of a hill just to the west of Kimpton. We had hunted slowly along the hedgerow at the bottom: bushes rustled soggily, partridges exploded indignantly, rabbits scuttled fleetingly, but nothing actually got up and ran. We had made our way through the scrub up the side of the field with the same lack of results. Now we started back along the top and every step took us nearer to the end of the day and of the season. I looked down at the long expanse of wet, grey plough. 'Somewhere out there,' I said to myself, 'there may well be a hare, crouching in the earth, and if there is, I am going to find him.' I left the others, squelched out to the middle of the field, and started to make my way along it; Rebecca came with me, and hunted on in front. Billy and his master hunted along the edge, about fifty yards to our right. I suppose we had gone three hundred yards, and were fifty yards from the end, when it happened. Does one hear a hare move before one sees it, or vice versa? I can distinctly remember hearing the thud of its feet as it shot across the plough. It had got up just to my right, and it headed back across the field behind us. I let out the most horrific scream; Rebecca turned and flew in pursuit. Over on the right Billy's head went up: the hare turned right-handed; Rebecca turned after it; Billy shot like a bullet straight in front of me, on course to intercept; the hare saw him, accelerated, and got by; Billy turned, Rebecca caught up, and together they hurled themselves across the ground. They were nearly on him when he reached the kale, into which he sank without trace; Billy charged in after him; Rebecca's head went up and she fell back. The kale heaved, swayed, and rattled; the hare flew out the other side, followed closely by Billy; Rebecca saw them and joined in again, and the three animals bolted into the tall, thorny undergrowth of the hillside opposite. Somewhere in that tangle Billy lost the trail, and Rebecca found it; she went off up the slope, while he galloped out onto the track and collapsed in a heaving, panting heap. He had run himself to a standstill. Naturally, I pointed this out to his owner as we trotted up to where he lay. (I was in about the same state of exhaustion as Billy, whereas his owner, who is extremely fit, was hardly blowing at all.) 'He can't be tired already, can he?' I asked. Then I speculated about how far the hare would get before Rebecca caught her, and whether she would bring it back or eat it on the spot. He became quite petulant, and angrily reminded me that Rebecca was the first one to give up the hunt when they got to the kale. We trudged to the top of the hill; after a few minutes Rebecca appeared and headed towards us. 'As I thought,' said I, viewing her from a distance. 'I see blood on her mouth. I suppose she's eaten it. What a greedy girl.' Billy's man was not amused. As it turned out, I laughed too soon; when Rebecca joined us, we found that one of her eyes was a mass of blood. She had been hit by a branch or a thorn, and had to go to the vet immediately. For a week, she had to have cream squeezed in her eye every day, which she didn't enjoy, and it was a month before she was given a clean bill of health.

Well, there you have it: a lousy day, a lovely hunt, and the hare was the winner. If only he had kept going the other way, across the field, he'd never have got to cover, and they might have caught him; but, as Billy's man pointed out, in that case the dogs would have had a murderous run across all that wet plough, with who-knows-what results. Besides, we both agreed that it was the biggest, best hare that either of us had seen all year, so why shouldn't it get away? Myself, I was quite happy (apart from the eye business) that Rebecca had at last had a good hunt with another dog. Roll on next year!

I feel I ought to confess that when I came to type out these last two chapters, I was tempted to indulge in a bit of fiction. "What about the perfect ending?" I asked myself "Surely no reader is going to be satisfied unless there is a whopping great climax, a technicolour sunset, and the Massed Bands of the Highland Brigade?" The germ of an idea nudged away at the back of my mind and then burst into full flower: what about amalgamating the Beloved's course with Billy's course? That way one would have Rebecca and Billy, the Beloved and me, a double-length course after a super-natural hare, ending in the best kill of all time. This could be followed by a feast for forty or so people (the hare, naturally, providing for all of them), and then the Beloved and I (not forgetting Rebecca) could flip-flap off into the sunset to the sound of the pipes. I must admit that I thought about it seriously and at length. In the end I came to the conclusion that anyone who had read the preceding chapters would not be fooled; after so much "real life" fiction would stick out like a sore thumb. Besides, I don't think Rebecca would much like being involved in a fairy tale: she's a very down-to-earth sort of person. So I dropped the idea and kept close to the truth, nearly all the truth, and practically nothing but the truth.

29

I must tell you what happened today.

There I was at Salisbury races, being jostled stupid by
an enormous crowd that had only come to see the ladies'
race, when a familiar face said 'Hello' and asked after
Rebecca. By means of a lightning burst of profound
reflection I identified him as the owner of Rebecca's
brother, the beautiful Nomad. We chatted in friendly
fashion: yes, Nomad was scheduled to reappear at the
Lurcher show, and would defend his title; yes, he was
likely to triumph again, because he was even handsomer
than last year, and because this year two of the judges
(not just one) had been involved in his ancestry; yes, he
had done some pretty smart coursing during the winter;
he had been here, and there, and he had even had
two days coursing with Mr Mills' dogs. 'One day,' he
confided with a happy smile, 'we killed nine hares in a
morning.'

'Blimey,' said I, somewhat wistful, somewhat melan-
choly, envious even. 'Rebecca only caught nine hares in
the whole Winter.' 'Still,' I added pathetically, 'she did
catch them all on her own, which was quite good, I suppose.'

'On her own?' He could scarcely get the words out,
because his mouth had fallen open, and seemed bent on
staying that way for some time. 'On her own? With no

other dogs to help her? How incredible! How marvellous! How wonderful! Nomad only actually caught one on his own.'

One moment he was floating contentedly on a cloud of satisfaction; the next, he was crawling, crippled, through the debris of his shattered illusions.

Seeing as how he is a nice fellow, I made it easy for him, and didn't rub it in too much; but I loved it, I really loved it.

Postscript

Rebecca is now an adult dog, and to prove it she has 'come in season' and gone to kennels for three weeks; which is why I have had the time and the peace to complete this volume. Soon after her departure, a reluctant policeman hove up the drive at breakfast time, and delivered the doleful news that summonses were being taken out against the owners of several dogs on the place, the charge being cattle-chasing. My spirits sank, and I endeavoured to hide behind an upright slice of toast; cattle-chasing is one of Rebecca's favourite forbidden sports; there are those who aver that it was she who introduced it to the neighbourhood; every previous complaint (they had only complained previously, never summonsed) had invariably culminated in some bitter allusion to 'that blue-eyed bitch' or even 'that wall-eyed whippet'. Imagine my delight (tinged with guilt, I must admit) when it became apparent that the incident in question had occurred while the evil one was in the sanctuary of her kennels. I sat up, looked the policeman straight in the eye, smiled smugly, and buttered the toast. God is on our side, I reflected; which being the case, there must be a good chance that Rebecca and I will live happily ever after.